HEROES OF CARENTAN

Denis van den Brink

I0891707

HEIMDAL

Preface by Thomas Rice, C/501st 101st Airborne Division

The last hero of La Barquette

The awareness of danger makes you think!

For me, Carentan is important because that's where I became "a seasoned paratrooper fighter". All our officers graduated from West Point with theoretical training. They taught us the ancestral art of war: grabbing fish by hand and frightening saber-toothed tigers!

During our daily training sessions, our officers constantly put us through simulated situations of danger and chaos, to the point that we couldn't wait to go to combat. We developed important qualities during our training: physical fitness, sleep resistance, attention to our comrades, sharing all our possessions, including letters, and courage. We placed these virtues in the most remote parts of our brains, where men rarely go, and we kept them for ourselves.

We endured and got through the combat thanks to all the important things we learned during training. When I jumped into Normandy, I was ready, and I reminded myself of all these virtues as I jumped.

As soon as I left the plane, I found myself in mortal danger and in a chaotic situation, hanging onto the door of the C-47, which was flying too low for me to jump. This experience taught me for the rest of my life that I will always be in dangerous and chaotic situations, and that I must constantly remind myself of the significant virtues I learned in training that allowed me to come through.

Once on the ground, near Carentan, I found myself on the front line, leading patrols. We were from the most exclusive family imaginable, as we were of the elite and well-trained. Nobody wanted lead to patrols. I felt like I was the tip of a sword, strong, thanks to my training, opening up the way. It also prepared me for the hard combat to come.

Combat gave the impression of being a game played by soldiers. It was like a game of dice, or cops and robbers, cat and mouse. We were there to drive out the occupier, and if he refused to leave, we had to catch him and kill him. The Germans said, "Let's laugh today, and kill tomorrow!" We answered: "We kill today, and laugh tomorrow!"

I came back from Normandy and Carentan with a rich experience. I can, at any time, remember the important things stored in my mind, and thus bear and overcome all situations in life. What happens in combat is very similar to the turpitudes of life, and the wisdom learned in combat makes life bearable.

After the war, many could not even talk about it. Some went away, others tried to forget everything and never tried to keep the important virtues we had learned.

When I returned from the army, I got rid of all my military gear, changed my way of expressing myself, and had a second meeting with my destiny; teaching. I have no regrets for the days I have lived. I was still young, 24 years old at the end of the conflict. And yet I had considerable experience in the art of combat.

We were not a band of savages who came to conquer and rob the French of their wealth. We simply reimbursed the gifts of Liberty, Equality, and Fraternity brought to us by Lafayette and Rochambeau.

Let us never forget
Thomas M. Rice

Foreword

Little-known, and misunderstood, the liberation of Carentan in June 1944 is not just a footnote among the thousand and one great military exploits of the Normandy Landings or the Battle of Normandy. From 9 to 13 June 1944, it was characterized by fighting of a rare ferocity and on a scale similar to that of a full-on battle, in both complexity and the extent of the means deployed by both German and American belligerents in the taking and defending of this town that was strategically positioned between the two American beachheads of Omaha and Utah Beach. Carentan was situated between the two US Army Corps, the Vth of General Leonard Townsend Gerow and the VIIth of General Joseph "Lightning Joe" Lawton Collins, at the gates of the lower Cotentin marshes.

The taking of Carentan was not an initial D-Day objective of the 101st Airborne Division, whose four regiments were first of all meant to secure the approaches to Utah Beach and facilitate the landing of the 4th Infantry Division, blocking all German attempts to access the beachhead. It was not until the evening of June 8, 1944, after the capture of Saint-Côme-du-Mont, that the US high command, with Eisenhower and Bradley, realized that the Screaming Eagles had a continuous front along the Douve river against Carentan and were thus in an ideal situation to attack and take the city. General Maxwell Davenport Taylor, commander of the 101st Airborne used his entire division, theoretically comprising of 14,200 men, with its four airborne regiments, (502nd, 506th, 501st PIR, 327/401st GIR) but also all its support units; the four airborne artillery batteries, its engineers (326th AEB), medical units, and logistics brought in by sea ... to encircle the city and drive out the stubborn *FJ Reg. 6*, the German parachutists of Major Friedrich von der Heydte.

Decimated, exhausted, and short of ammunition, the *Fallschirmjäger* finally evacuated the city during the night of June 11 to 12, but only to return there in the afternoon of 12 June with the support of an entire armored division, the *17. SS "Götz von Berlichingen"*. The clash took an epic turn on June 13 with the arrival of the American cavalry prefigured in this case by Combat Command A of the 2nd US Armored Division. The Shermans of General Maurice Rose ferociously attacked the self-propelled guns and the German grenadiers along the roads of Auvers and Périers to free Carentan once and for all from German grip. Military casualties, both German and American, were considerable, but the town and its inhabitants also suffered terribly. The US Navy and its big cruisers USS Quincy and USS Texas fired on the town continuously on the night of June 11, inflicting terrible losses and destruction on the city.

These military feats deserve a thorough examination so that the scale, the strategic importance and the sacrifices made do not fall into oblivion. Better than a chronological narrative, the living testimonies of the actors of the battle make it possible to locate and see the numerous exploits which make up the battle of Carentan. Shortly after midnight on June 6, 1944, 6,670 paratroopers belonging to the 101st Airborne were dispersed over a vast area of nearly 30 km^2, including the town of Carentan, Valognes to Saint Georges du Bohon, and sometimes even to the gates of Cherbourg for the unfortunate gunners of the 377th PFAB. The rest of the division arrived partly by gliders, but mostly by sea landing at Utah Beach. Each personal story is an epic in itself. This book modestly gathers a handful of these individual adventures, shedding a deeply human light on what was the complexity and violence of the struggles for the liberation of Lower Cotentin and Carentan.

101st Airborne Division flag presented to the town of Carentan in the 1950s...

(1) The fighting of the *Fallschirmjäger* commanded by von der Heydte, can be read in the Lions de Carentan, Heimdal.

Witnesses to history...

This new publication joins the long list of books published by Editions Heimdal, a publisher that was founded in 1975 and which has gained an international reputation over the last forty years for its books covering the Landings and the Battle of Normandy. The Carentan area played a determining role. As early as the Middle Ages, the town, which at that time was fortified, was the only gateway between the Bessin, to the east, the Saint-Lô area, to the south-east, and the Cotentin peninsula (1).

On 6 June 1944, this peninsula was in the middle of the marshlands that had been flooded by the Germans and was thus a determining position to link-up the airborne bridgehead and Utah Beach to the landing sector of Omaha Beach. Also, Hitler's intuition concerning an allied landing in the "*Cherbourg and Cotentin peninsula*" sector (2), had led him to strengthen this sector by bringing in the *352. Infanterie-Division* south of the future Omaha Beach sector – a division whose presence was not picked up by the Allies -, but also the *91. Luftflande-Division*, into the heart of the Cotentin Peninsula, forcing the Allies to modify their plans. Indeed, one of the two US airborne divisions was initially due to be dropped to the west of the peninsula. But, above all, concerning the subject that interests us here, a parachutist regiment, *Fallschirmjäger-Regiment 6,* led by Major Friedrich baron von der Heydte, had been transferred there from Germany on 11 May 1944, less than four weeks before D-Day. They were stationed south-west of Carentan, near the *91. Luftflande-Division*, to whom they depended on for supplies (3). The Regiment's HQ was then at Gonfreville, north of Périers, the *I.Bataillon* (*Hauptmann* Emil Preikschat), in the region of Saint-Jores and Mont Castre, the *II.Bataillon* (*Hauptmann* Rolf Mager), near Lessay, and the *III.Bataillon* (*Hauptmann* Trebes), between Carentan and Périers. Thus, these German reinforcements which arrived a short time before the Landings, would be the toughest opponents for the American expeditionary corps of D-Day. At Omaha Beach, without the *352.ID*, the thin curtain of *716. ID* troops would have been quickly brushed aside, leaving an almost gaping front line nearly as far as Saint-Lô. In the Cotentin, the *91.LD* greatly complicated matters for the mission of the airborne troops, with the latter having to fight for La Fière, Pont-l'Abbé et Saint-Sauveur-le-Vicomte.

Von der Heydte's paras would be particularly formidable adversaries. Without them, the taking of Carentan would have been a formality and the *Götz von Berlichingen* mechanized division, which arrived later, would have been halted much further south. Thus, the "Battle of Carentan" became something of an epic encounter as it was a fight between elite troops: those of the USA with the 101st Airborne

This exceptional photo was taken on 17 May 1944, during an inspection by field-marshal Rommel in the Cotentin, less than three weeks before D-Day. He is visiting *Fallschirmjäger-Regiment 6,* when in fact he had come to inspect the *91.Luftlande-Division* of general Wilhelm Falley, considered as being vital to the foreseen invasion... This division, a tank battalion - *Panzer-Abteilung 100* which would intervene at the La Fière bridge — and von der Heydte's paras, were reinforcements that had arrived less than a month before the Landings, following an intuition on Hitler's part and his subsequent orders. Indeed, he was the only one to believe in the possibility of landings in Normandy and had succeeded in convincing Rommel, faced with the inertia... or collusion in favor of the Allies, for some, of the German high command. In this photo we can see field-marshal Rommel meeting the three battalion commanders of the 6th parachute regiment with, from left to right: *Hauptmann* Rolf Mager *(Kdr. II battalion*, awarded the Knight's Cross of the Iron Cross on 31 October 1944, died 1 January 1942), wearing his double cuff title (Afrika and Kreta) on the left sleeve of his camouflage jump smock, *Oberleutnant* Helmut Wagner *(Kdr.* 9th company and awarded the Knight's Cross on 24 January 1942 – killed by artillery fire at Saint-Côme-du-Mont, 7 June), and an unidentified *Leutnant*, wearing the Kreta cuff title on his camouflage smock. Standing behind field-marshal Rommel is *Hauptmann* Horst Trebes, *Kommandeur* of the II battalion, wearing the Knight's Cross of the Iron Cross at his neck, awarded on 9 July 1941 for his rôle in the Crete campaign, killed in Normandy on 29 July. These men are veterans and exceptional officers, elite soldiers who are preparing to encounter other elite combatants in a fight that will go down in history...(Private collection)

paratroopers, and those of Germany with the 6th regiment's paras. It was a ferocious battle between the best, with the outnumbered *Fallschirmjäger* fielding less than two battalions after their disaster at Hell's Corner, and low on ammunition, being forced to withdraw, acquiring the nickname 'The Lions of Carentan'. It was in fighting these combatants that the American paratroopers covered themselves in military glory leading to the capture of the town where, a few centuries earlier, medieval monarchs such as Henry II Plantagenet or John, King of England, had stayed!

Finally, we should salute this work by Denis Van den Brink who, with this book, has gathered together some exceptional eye-witness accounts in a series of portraits which add to the editorial policy of our publishing company concerning this sector, firstly with Objective Carentan (4), which remains the book that provides a chronological summary of the fighting. This new book is an indispensable addition to the latter. Just as indispensable are the two books by Mark Bando, which give a more overall view but which were written by an author who met hundreds 101st Airborne veterans (5). Finally, we should also remember the valiant adversaries of the "Screaming Eagles" with the book, "The Lions of Carentan" (6). Thus, you will have all the necessary reading required for this battle. This new publication was made possible by the numerous contacts that Denis van den Brink maintained with veterans, the dwindling number of which remain the final witnesses.

George Bernage,
historian and publisher

(1) See *Vikland* n°28, which covers Carentan, the medieval town, Heimdal, February 2019.

(2) Mentioned as early as 1948 by Basil H. Liddell Hart, in a book published in English and translated into French at the time and which has recently been republished – see pages 462 to 468 of The German generals talk.

(3) See p. 31 of the book *The Lions of Carentan*, Heimdal, 2005, by Volker Griesser.

(4) Georges Bernage, *Objective Carentan*, Editions Heimdal, 2010, 2nd edition: 2016.

(5) Mark Bando, *The 101st Airborne Division In the Second World War, "Vanguard of the Crusade"*. Heimdal, 2012 and 2nd edition: 2018, and *The secret story of the 101st Airborne Division, "Avenging Eagles"*, Heimdal, 2014.

(6) Temporarily out of print.

SUMMARY

When it was activated in August 1942, the 101st Airborne Division decided to use as its emblem the American eagle of the 101st Division that was at the time a National Guard unit. It was inspired by the 8th Wisconsin regiment's mascot, ancestor of the 101st Division, and which was followed into combat during the Civil War by Old Abe, an American bald eagle. The new 101st Airborne Division immediately got its own mascot, an eagle that was named Young Abe, and which mysteriously died a short time afterwards.

1. Night paratroopers

Major General Maxwell Davenport Taylor, Commander-in-Chief of the 101st Airborne Division. The diplomatic General!

Born August 26, 1901 in Keynesville, a small town in north central Missouri, Maxwell Davenport Taylor was an only son. His father was a lawyer for a railroad company. He was brought up on stories of the Civil War told by his maternal grandfather who had fought for the Confederation. "*At 5 years old*," he later wrote, "*I decided to go to West Point.*" Taylor was a great speaker in his early years at Northeast High School in Kansas City, where he graduated at the age of 15. He then entered Kansas City Junior College. This is where he sat exams for the United-States Military Academy and Naval Academy. Although brilliant at Latin, Greek and Spanish, his knowledge of geography was too limited and he failed the entrance exam in Annapolis. He later said: "*If the Strait of Malacca had been in Europe, I would have been an Admiral rather than General.*" At West Point, he was a cadet with the rank of captain, editor of the student paper, and graduated in 1922, the youngest cadet in his class and 4th in academic results. 2nd Lieutenant in the Engineering Corps, he joined the Virginia Engineering School the following year, before being assigned to Maryland, Hawaii and Washington. In the years following the First World War, before the United States decided to rearm, promotion was slow in the regular army. With the rank of Lieutenant, he was transferred to the 10th Artillery in 1926, and did not reach the rank of captain until 1935.

Previously noticed as being a brilliant officer, he was sent to Paris where he perfected his French. Upon his return, he was appointed to West Point as a French and Spanish teacher. After two years at the Fort Leavenworth Command and General Staff School, he was posted to the US Embassy in Tokyo to learn Japanese. In 1939, he was a military attaché in Beijing. After a course at the Army War College in June 1940, he accompanied General Matt Ridgway on inspection in nine Latin American countries, and was appointed to lead an artillery battalion. At the declaration of war, he was Chief of Staff to Ridgway, with the rank of Colonel. In December 1942, he became Brigadier General and commanded the artillery of a famous division... the 82nd Airborne, with which he landed in North Africa in May 1943.

At the end of September 1942, Matt Ridgway, Commanding Officer of the new 82nd Airborne, decided to inspect his paratrooper regiment, the 504th PIR at Fort Benning. He also decided that it was time for him to face the particularity of his division – parachute jumps! All of his staff volunteered – Joe Swing, Bud Miley (CDA) Doc Eaton, Bill Moorman, Don Faith, Ridgway's historic aide... and Maxwell Davenport Taylor, Division Artillery Commander. The future Commanding Officer of 101st AB, simply hated it, "*I must have been drunk when I volunteered for this jump!*" Julian Ewell, future CO of the 3/501st, jumpmaster during this jump at Benning, who jumped right after Taylor, said that his boss has landed... "*head first!*"

All in all, it seems that Max Taylor made only three jumps during the Second World War. After this first jump stateside, he made his second jump in combat in Normandy, then in Holland during Ope-

Below: Major General Maxwell Davenport Taylor, photographed sometime around June 20th along the wet dock in Carentan where the 101st Airborne Division headquarters personnel took refuge from persistent German shelling.

Below, right: When he was still only a Brigadier General and artillery commander of the 82nd Airborne, Max Taylor led a secret mission in Rome in September 1943 to evaluate Italian intentions and the possibility of an airborne operation over Rome (Operation Giant II). A few weeks later he would receive the official Italian surrender from marshal Badoglio.

ration Market. For Normandy, he took off from Weltford Park aboard the No. 13 serial plane, 435th TCG, Lt. Col Frank Mc Neese commanding, and pilot of the plane. Max Taylor had with him 7 MPs, his radio Operator George Koskimaki, his aide-de-camp, and a medic. The jumpmaster was the G-43 division, Major Lawrence "Larry" Legere, who was later seriously wounded in Pouppeville. Reuters News Agency correspondent Robert Reuben was on the trip. Qualified parachutist Chilton Foliat also jumped in Normandy. Taylor became at this moment in history the first general to jump during an operation. Three curious details mark this second jump of the historic leader of the 101st Airborne: He took a small inflatable mattress, and was able to take a nap during the flight. He also took a bottle of good whiskey in his bag. A few days before the jump, he played a racket ball game with his old friend, Colonel Frank "Froggie" Reed... and seriously injured a tendon in his foot. As a consequence, he landed on only his left leg in Normandy, and limped during the first week of the invasion...

Gerald J. Higgins, Assistant Division Commander; 101st Airborne

Gerald Joseph Higgins, West Point Class 1934, was born August 29, 1909. He is one of those overlooked men, a soldier in the shadows, whose contribution to history is nevertheless considerable. Historians agree that it was he, in close collaboration with William Carey Lee, then with Max Taylor, who forged the 101st Airborne. His career was amazing. He entered West Point without any preparation as an other rank from the regular army. Ten years later, he became a General! He began his career at Presidio in 1937 as Commanding Officer, 30th Infantry Regiment with the rank of captain. This is where he answered a call for volunteers for the paratroopers.

He joined the 501st Parachute Infantry Battalion in February 41. He became one of the pioneers of the US Airborne. In December of the same year, he joined the Provisional Parachute Group, ancestor of the Airborne Command, under the command of Bill Lee. His career took off at a dizzy pace.

April 42: G-3 (Operations) Airborne Command at Fort Bragg

August 16 42: G-3 101st Airborne at Claibourne, Lt Colonel

March 43, Chief of Staff 101st Airborne

June 44, Assistant Division Commander, replacing Don Pratt, killed on D.Day. He supplanted Sink and Johnson, both 101st regimental commanders, who were older than him.

August 44; became Brigadier General aged 34, the youngest in the entire US Army to hold this position, appointed by Taylor. Taylor later said, *"This was the worst decision of my career that I have never regretted..."* The job should have gone to senior colonels or generals, but Higgins had done a great job in Normandy...

General Gerald Higgins was made Assistant Division Commander following Don Pratt's tragic death on 6 June 1944, in spite of his young age, 34, and the seniority of such highly qualified officers as Robert Sink, Howard Johnson or Anthony McAuliffe.

Gerald Higgins, a 34-year old brigadier general, seen here at the beginning of Operation Market.

Charles H. Young
No airborne without troop carriers

Charles H. Young was born in Argonia, Kansas in 1914. He was the boss of the 439th Troop Carrier Group, which notably dropped part of the 506th PIR in Normandy (based at Upottery, 1/506th and 2/506th), but which was also involved in all the major airborne operations of the war.

The 439th consisted of the Group Head Squadron, the 91st Troop Carrier Squadron (C-47 L4), the 92nd Troop Carrier Squadron (C-47 J8), the 93rd Troop Carrier Squadron (C-47 3B) and the 94th Troop Carrier Squadron (C-47 D8), based in Balderton, Nottinghamshire then Upottery, Devonshire.

Coming from a family of farmers, Charles Young began his career as a pilot at the age of 21 with field fertilization operations from an OX-5 Powered American Eagle. He was accepted into the US Army Air Corps Flying Cadets at Randolph Field in 1936, just after graduating from Philipps University of Enid, Oklahoma. He still holds the USAF record for the minimum time spent flying with an instructor before flying solo – 55 minutes! He next spent two years at Kelly Fields in the 90th Attack Squadron, commanded at the time by the huge Paul L. Williams, who later became CO of the IX Troop Carrier Command.

In September 1939, Young returned to civilian life and entered American Airlines as a pilot. He was recalled in 1942 to participate in the organization of Troop Carriers. He was one of the original executives of the First Troop Carrier Command. In January 44 he took command of the 439th Troop Carrier Group. At 30, he was the youngest Troop Carrier commander. At the controls of his C-47,

Below: Charles Young at Uppotery airfield with boxing champion Joe Louis.

Above: The IX Troop Carrier Command was constituted on 11 October 1943(activated October 16th) in England under 9th Air Force supervision. It included the 50th, 52nd and 53rd Troop Carrier Wings and was commanded in June 1944 by Major General Paul Williams. These units operated C-47 aircraft and gliders to transport troops.

Right: Lt. Colonel Charles Young at the controls of his aircraft "Argonia", C-47 N° 43-15159, leading airplane of the the 439th TCG on D-Day, with his co-pilot 1st Lt. Adam Parsons.

the Argonia, he was one of the first over Normandy in the early hours of June 6, 1944 to drop the 1/506th and 2/506th. 80 C-47s formed the 439th TCG from Upottery

He went on to be a leading pilot on all major war operations, including tough resupply missions in Belgium and Germany. He joined American Airlines after the war and remained with this company for 35 years. He is the author of a book that is a reference concerning the Troop Carriers, "Into the Valley!".

His plane, the C 47 Argonia N ° 315159 is represented at the Airborne Museum of Sainte-Mère-Eglise. In reality, it is C-47 No. 42-100825, 92nd Squadron, 439th TC Group, the second serial D-Day, chalk No. 49, piloted by 1st Lt Charles H. Imschweiler. On June 7, it was involved in the towing of Horsa gliders with the 439th TCG. It played a part in Operation Dragoon on August 15 in Provence, and Holland for Market. It is also said to have towed two Wacos to the assault on Wesel on 24 March 1945. Having served in French naval aviation from 1962, it was handed over to the Parachute Friendship League, on the initiative of the Airborne Museum of Sainte-Mère-Eglise on 1 September 1981. It was restored in the colors of Argonia, C-47 No. 43-15159, the 439th TCG's leading aircraft on D-Day, commanded by Charles Young.

Harold Eugene Sellers, F/501st Infantry Parachute, Pathfinder 101st Airborne

Harold E. "Gene" Sellers is one of the characters honored by the short introductory film shown at the Visitor's Center of the Omaha Beach Cemetery in Colleville. "Gene" was a freshman at the University of Arkansas and on a scholarship as he played in the school's US football team. Nevertheless, he decided to sign up and chose the paratroops. He was dispatched to 1st platoon, F company, 501st PIR, which would, in January 1944, be attached to the 101st Airborne. He was a volunteer in early April 1944 for a brand new provisional unit, the Pathfinders, scouts responsible for marking out the jump zones. Leonard Newcomb of F/501 was in his tent at Hampstead Marshall early February 44 when his company's Executive Officer told him about the Pathfinders. Newcomb looked at his pals Rob Larsen and Joe Bass and the three men nodded. Harold Sellers, coming to pick up his mail, then entered. Seeing that his squad buddies were up to something, and without really knowing what it was, Sellers said, "*Count me in*". He was sent to the North Witham airfield and joined the 2/501st Pathfinder team (plane chalk N ° 7, of which there is no photo – author's note). His serial had to jump on the terrible DZ "D" that the Germans had covered with their firepower. He dropped to the south east of St-Côme-du-Mont, not far from the Dead Man's Corner, literally in front of the barrel of a MG 42. He was killed in his harness before even touching the ground. It was 00:44 hrs on Tuesday, June 6, 1944. He shares the sad privilege of probably being the first American KIA (D-Day) with another 501st trooper, Pvt Stanley S. Suwarsky of 3/501st, Plane No. 6, DZ "C", also killed when he landed near Sainte-Marie-du-Mont, at exactly the same time.

Stanley S. Suwarsky.

Below: Gene Sellers volunteered for pathfinders duty in April 1944, out of friendship for his tent buddies at Hamstead Marshall. An Arkansas University student, his future looked bright. He was to become one of the first Screaming Eagles killed in action on D-Day.

Don McDougall.

Sellers.

WHAT WAS A PATHFINDER?

Contrary to many preconceived ideas, a Pathfinder was not only an elite soldier (all the paratroopers were) but, above all, a technician, a communications expert who mastered Morse code perfectly, as well as the techniques painstakingly developed after March 1943 under the combined efforts of Airborne Command, Troop Carrier Transport pilots, and "bad drop specialists" of 2/509 GDP. To allow them to perform in record time, in the right place and without enemy intervention during their work of identification and marking of the Drop Zone and Landing Zone, these soldier-technicians were accompanied by "security men", also trained in the use of marking instruments, but more specifically dedicated to eliminating any enemy who came to obstruct the work of pathfinders. Less well-known are the "follow up" Pathfinders who were brought in with the very first serials and able, in event of failure, capture or elimination of the Pathfinders, to take over and emit signals towards the C-47s of the invasion fleet.

Three men were instrumental in the creation of the Pathfinders school – Capt. Bill Kirkpatrick (313 TCG), Capt. Jack Norton (505) and Capt. Frank Boyd (376th PFAB). Norton caught malaria and it was Boyd who was tasked with carrying out experimental trials. The Army Air Force pathfinders school was first established at Cottesmore in February 44, and the Airborne pathfinders school was started up at North Witham near Grantham in March.

The school took in Lillyman's "volunteers", plus those from the 101st Airborne and the Ninth Troop Carrier Command Pathfinder Group of Lt Colonel Joel Crouch, a pioneer of pathfinder work from North Africa and Italy. Each of the three 82nd Airborne Regiments, the 505th, 507th and 508th PIR, sent 6 officers and 54 men, all selected from volunteers. In total, more than 350 US and British men worked at this school before the invasion of Normandy. Pathfinders learned how to use their transmitter tools, including long-wave radios, eureka-rebecca equipment, smoke signals, holophane panels, fluorescent panels for daytime ground marking and T-shaped wind direction indicators.

Before D-Day, the composition of a pathfinders team was modified as follows:

- 2 officers and 12 men (Team Leader, Team Leader Assistant, Light section leader, seven men, two Eureka operators and two Eureka operator assistants.

- One team per battalion, or three teams of pathfinders per regiment, flying in a V-shaped formation of three aircraft to their DZ.

As the training progressed, the team structure changed, going up to two officers and 12 men, plus a security team of 5 men. A pathfinder team was thus composed as follows:

Team leader, assistant team leader, Light section leader, seven "light men", two Eureka operators and two Eureka assistant operators, plus the team of security men.

For the record, pathfinders' passwords were different from those used by the bulk of paratroopers, (Flash-Thunder-Welcome). The scouts used "Boise", to which the response was "Idaho".

Troop carrier personnel were the first to wear pathfinder patches as early as May 1944. Later on, all paratroopers attending pathfinder school in North Witham were allowed, whether they jumped or not, to wear this patch on the left sleeve.

Foucarville, the US paratroopers' bluff

In the spring of 1944, the village of Foucarville was occupied by the 1st battalion of *Grenadier-Regiment 919* (*709. Infanterie-Division*) commanded by *Hauptmann* Fink who set up his command post there. The town was located north of the "A" coded jump zone designated by the Americans for the drop of the 502nd Parachute Infantry Regiment commanded by Colonel George van Horn Moseley. This regiment, via the 1st Battalion led by Lieutenant Colonel Patrick F. Cassidy, was responsible for securing the northernmost highways connecting Utah Beach and inland through the wide flooded marshes. The 1st Battalion of the 502nd Parachute Infantry Regiment (PIR) was not dropped at the planned location, but American paratroopers moved towards their targets without delay. Several airborne units became mixed up due to these bad drops: approximately 180 paratroopers belonging to the 2nd Battalion of the 506th PIR gathered in the night near Foucarville. They were joined by around 20 paratroopers from the 508th PIR (82nd Airborne Division) and at 3:30 am by Lieutenant-Colonel Robert L. Strayer, commanding the 2nd Battalion of the 506th PIR accompanied by around fifty other paratroopers. These elements joined forces and moved south at 4:30. Immediately south of Foucarville, before Saint-Germain-de-Varreville, they were attacked and pinned down by the enemy until noon. In order to cover the actions being led towards the causeways, a detachment

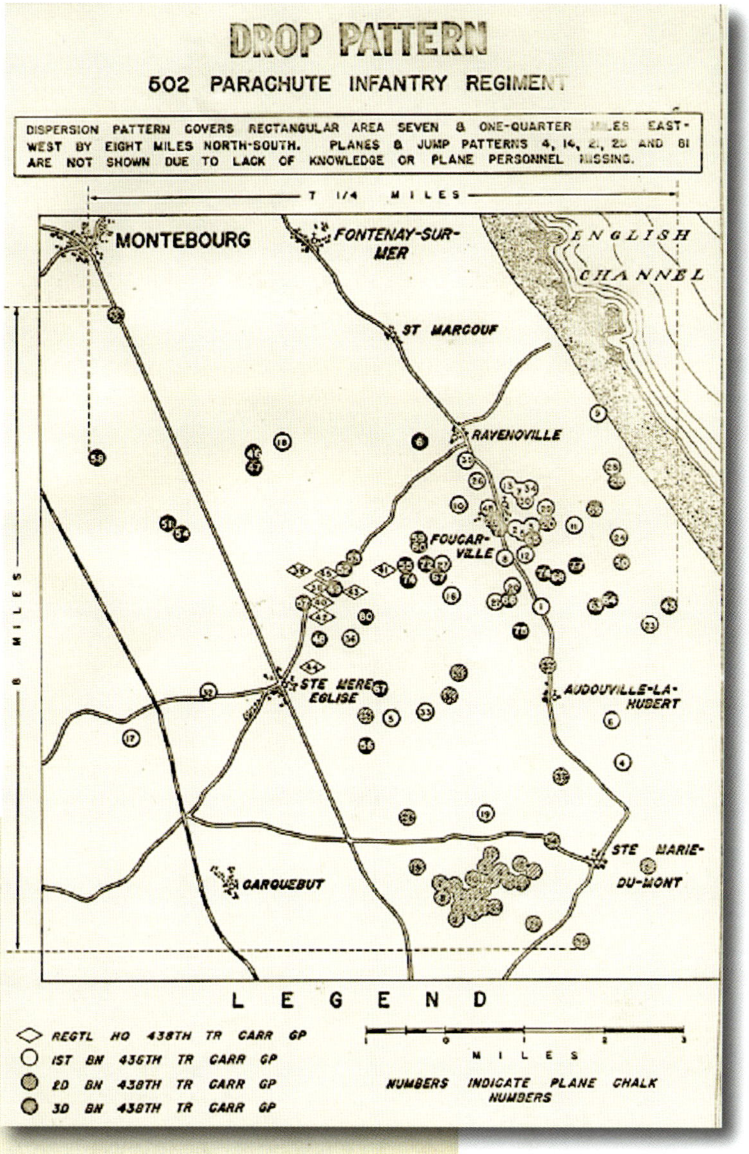

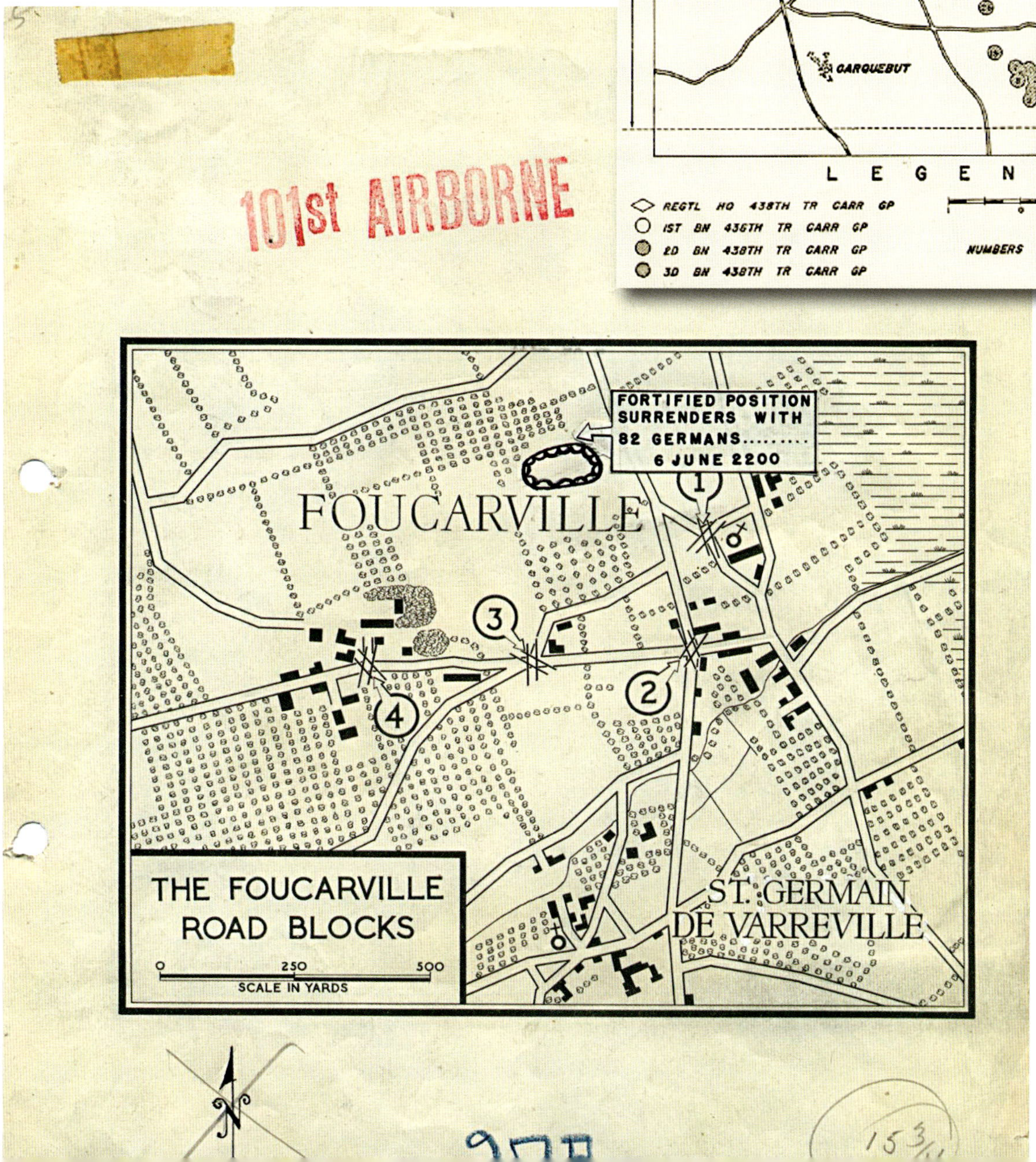

The 502nd Parachute Infantry took off from Membury and Greenham Common as the first wave of the airborne assault headed for Drop Zone A. Their objectives were the two northernmost causeways in Ravenoville and Saint-Martin-de-Varreville, as well as the Saint-Germain gun battery and its 122 mm guns.

of 45 soldiers of A Company, 502nd PIR, led by Lieutenant Wallace A. Swanson was sent to the area of Foucarville to block the departmental roads 17 and 14. Shortly after noon, "Swannie" set up four roadblocks. Meanwhile, the Germans deployed multiple reinforcements from the North Cotentin, notably *Sturm-Battalion AOK 7* and *Panzerjäger-Abteilung 709*. Four vehicles were spotted on the road between Beuzeville-au-Plain and Foucarville: they were stopped and destroyed thanks to the action of Lieutenant Swanson. At the end of the day, the northern outskirts of Foucarville were held by Swanson's men.

Foucarville, was thus the main German defense point, situated on a small fortified hill, with trenches and barbed wire. This is where the Germans concentrated all the prisoners taken during the night, these being 17 men from A and C Companies of 502 PIR. C Company of the 502nd attacked this "strong-point" during the day of the 6th with little success. Around 10 pm, the Germans surrendered en masse, while others tried to escape to the north. This surrender was due to a monumental bluff by the prisoners who reportedly informed the German command that a terrible artillery barrage, unleashed by the 377th PFAB, was due to hit Foucarville at 10.30 pm... The bluff worked and 82 (87 according to Koskimaki) Germans surrendered, including a French woman married to a German officer. In fear of being shot down, the Germans waved a white flag but did not show themselves. C Company moved on, followed by elements of the 4th ID. One of the paratroopers, Pfc Hewitt Tippits, was sent by the Germans to explain to the Americans that the garrison had surrendered. Tippits was a pure "Southerner", a guy from the south with a thick drawl. He screamed from the entrance of the dugouts, "*Don't shoot, I'm a yank! I'm a yank!*"... Coming from a southerner, the sentence was more than a little ironic and he became the laughing stock of his comrades until the end of the war. However, many German die-hards tried to flee north but the GI prisoners seized the weapons of the Germans that had surrendered and killed them. 50 German dead were counted... Pat Cassidy, CO of 1/502, would then lead his battalion, following Robert Cole's, in the assault along Purple Heart Lane between Saint-Côme-du-Mont and Carentan. His leadership under enemy fire when crossing bridges over the Douve on June 11 earned him the Distinguished Service Cross.

Lieutenant Bernard Bucior was jumpmaster of his C-47 on D-Day. He helped eliminate various fortified German positions in the Foucarville area. Seriously wounded in action shortly afterwards, he was evacuated to Utah Beach and put on board LST N° 283.

The Bucior mystery, B/502 PIR

July 1944; Irene Bucior of Cape Elizabeth, Maine learned that her brother, Lieutenant Bernard G. "B.G." Bucior, was listed as Missing In Action in Normandy. Bucior, a professional golf coach at Wethersfield Country Club, signed up in September 41 at the age of 21. He quickly joined the paratroops and embarked for Europe with the 502 PIR. His disappearance would be described as one of the great mysteries of D-Day by the historian S.L.A. Marshall in his book "Night drop". 1st Lt Bucior was in Haut Fornel on the afternoon of June 7th with Captain Fred Hancock, CO of Company C. Two self-propelled 88 mm guns, with their crews, had just entered the small town and Hancock wanted these guns. He sent Bucior with 17 men to flank the enemy from the left, while Lt Borchert with 17 men made the same move on the right. Bucior came across a farm full of Germans. He posted a .30 cal. machine-gun to block them and continued his way to the guns. However, the Germans had anticipated his movement and, at a bend in a field, he came face to face with an 88 and thirty Germans. Bucior tried to retreat but was hit by a bullet that went through his shoulder. His men took him to the shelter and bandaged him. Bucior was not finished. He sent back his men to fight along the sunken roads. Clashes with enemy groups that had numerical superiority were multiplying. Bucior's men exhorted him to go back. "*Hell no! Hell no!*" Bucior replied angrily. The Germans surrounded the small group and brought down mortar fire. Bucior was wounded in six places. He finally resolved to leave. He got up but collapsed. He had only two able-bodied, yet wounded men with him. They carried him back. It was Pat Cassidy, CO of 1/502 who saw them dragging the inert but conscious body of Bucior across fields. Cassidy knew that the entire C Company was engaged. He had to carry on, albeit with a heavy heart due to having to leave his wounded men and not having the time to take care of them. No one would hear from Bucior. What happened to him between meeting Cassidy and Utah Beach? It was not until many years later that a certain Phil Shofner, wounded on June 6, one of Bucior's men, remembered talking to him at Utah, while Bucior was evacuated aboard a hospital ship. A few hours later, his ship hit a floating mine. A large number of wounded, including Bucior, were killed, and their bodies without dog tags, disappeared. This is how the name of Bernard Bucior appears on the MIA wall in Colleville. A month later, the body of Robert G. Hester was found near Le Havre. He was also from B/502, and on the same Hospital Ship as Bucior.

Left: Bernard Bucior, left, in Hungerford prior to D-Day.

Below: a Lt. Colonel in Normandy, in charge of planning, he fought a rifleman's war for over 7 days, cut-off behind enemy lines. He took his own life on 7 December 1944, a few days before the German offensive in the Ardennes. He was buried at the temporary American cemetery at Champigneul.

Bernard Bucior was of Polish extraction and his real name was Brouislaus. At 21, he was an accomplished athlete, brilliant swimmer, basketball player and pole vault specialist.

Lieutenant Colonel Raymond D. Millener, G-3, 101st Airborne, the helping hand of a lost officer...

Lt Colonel Raymond Davis "Bud" Millener, was G-3 (planning) for the 101st in Normandy, where he received his Distinguished Service Cross after being dropped west of Picauville. Millener had not yet finished his jump school. For several days, he fought in rearguard actions with a small group of soldiers from HQ/501st and the Signal Company. With his troops, he allegedly destroyed two tanks, two half-tracks and ambushed several German motorcycle dispatch riders and *kübelwagens*, as well as an ammunition convoy. These men managed to avoid capture and were eventually relieved by elements of the 90th ID in the Prétot area. Millener returned to the 101st headquarters when it was in Carentan.

On his way to Holland, as part of Operation Market, his plane was hit by the flak. He jumped from a flaming C-47 into the region of Eindhoven.

On December 7, 1944 in Mourmelon-le-Grand, he borrowed a razor from a Signal Corps soldier. He shaved quietly, then, standing in front of his mirror, placed his .45 in his mouth and pulled the trigger without leaving any explanation...

Three suicides were recorded in 5 days in Mourmelon from December 5th to 11th, 1944; a staff officer, a Master Sergeant (David Harmon) and the Assistant Chief of Staff of the Division, the Acting G-3, Lt Colonel Raymond D "Bud" Millener.

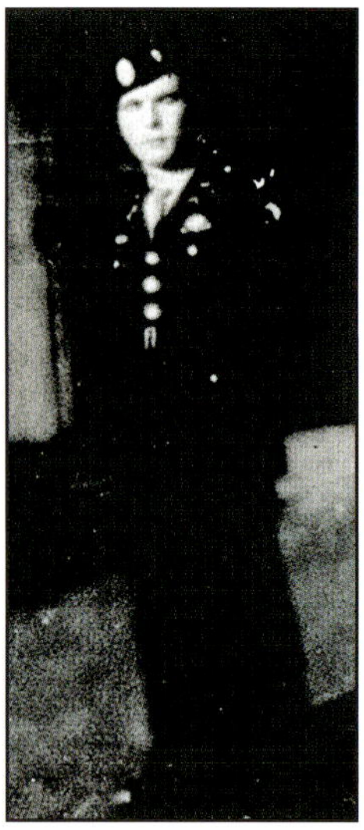

Lieutenant Brierre belonged to the 501st PIR Military Police platoon. He made history on 6 June 1944 at 11.10 am when linking up with 4th ID elements arriving from Utah Beach.

Lieutenant Eugene D. Brierre, C/501st, an MP, first contact between 4th ID and 101st Airborne

Assigned to the HQ MP platoon of the 101st Airborne, Lieutenant Brierre made history on June 6, 1944 at 11:10 am by making the first link up between airborne troops and the 4th ID that had landed at Utah Beach. The scene took place on a small bridge east of Pouppeville, and Brierre; with his group of 8 soldiers, linked-up with Captain George L. Mabry Jr., S-3, 3/8th Infantry. By the time the evening had come, Pouppeville was totally secure. Brierre walked around the village. He saw the half-open door of a small house. Out of curiosity, he went through the open door... and came face to face with the barrel of a Mauser. The weapon was held by a young German lying on the ground. The soldier was wounded. Brierre also pointed his weapon. The German dropped his rifle. His trembling hand pointed to something on a table. Brierre hesitated, not understanding. The German looked at him, his eyes strangely begging him for something. The American lowered his weapon, approached the table and saw a rosary. He took it and saw again the look of the weak and yet pleading German. Brierre put the rosary in his hand. The German seemed to relax. His head dropped and he closed his eyes. In the half-light Brierre could just see the slow movement of his fingers as he passed the rosary beads between them. Quietly, he left. He returned the next morning. The half-open door did not move. He glanced inside. The German was there, stretched out, his rosary in his hand. He was dead.

Captain George L. Mabry Jr.

Eugene D. Brierre was born on January 4, 1924 in New Orleans. He attended the Coast Guard Military Academy from 1933 to 1942. On June 12, 1942, he received his 2nd Lieutenant's commission and left for Camp Walters in Texas. Here, he volunteered for the paratroops. He was first assigned to the 506th PIR. Then in January 1944, in England, he joined C Company of the 501st PIR. Major Legere recruited him to lead a platoon of MPs in Normandy, with the mission of securing the headquarters of Max Taylor. He jumped as assistant jumpmaster from Taylor's plane.

Joseph Beyrle, from Saint-Côme-du-Mont to Moscow Item 506th Parachute Infantry, 101st Airborne

Joseph Beyrle (pronounced buy-early) was born in Muskegon, Michigan, in 1923, to Bavarian immigrant parents. Joe was an accomplished athlete who, in the fall of 1942, entered Notre Dame University with an athletics scholarship. Instead, he signed up for something new and unknown, the paratroopers. From there, Joe's fate would take a turn that the best Hollywood writers could not have imagined. Joe successfully went through Toccoa's tough selection, followed by his para training at Benning and received his wings at the beginning of 43. To his mother, who asked him how many times he had boarded the plane, he answered, *"I did 11 takeoffs... but no landings!"* In September 43, he joined Item Company, 506th Parachute Infantry Regiment, 101st Airborne in England. The training intensified and Joe loved jumping. In April 1944, he had more than 30 jumps to his credit, he was summoned one day to the

Lieutenant Nathan Marks was an original Geronimo, G Company platoon leader. He died during the fighting for Pouppeville, shot through the head by a German sniper.

office of Lt. Col Robert Wolverton, CO of 3/506. Two strange men in plain clothes attended the interview. They belonged to the secret services and were looking for an exceptional para for a secret mission. Joe agreed. In the greatest secrecy (nobody in his unit ever learned of it), Joe jumped somewhere in Brittany a month before the invasion to hand over a belt full of gold to the French Resistance. So here was this 21- year old, probably the first US soldier to touch French soil. He jumped through the trapdoor of a Lysander and, like in a movie, was picked up by French Resistance fighters who hid him, and then took him with extreme precautions, moving only at night, to a small port where he embarked on a small fishing boat and was picked up off the coast by the Royal Navy. He returned to his barracks and resumed training as if nothing had happened. Officially, he had gone to see his sick brother in a military hospital in the north of England. A few days later, it happened again, as he was again contacted by the secret services and made a second jump in France. It was the beginning of May and a para of the 506th had already jumped onto French soil twice.

June 6th came and Joe experienced the same anxieties and fears as the 6,600 paras of the division. He landed amidst flak fire on the roof of the Church of St. Côme-du-Mont. Alone and disoriented, he spent the night of D-Day crawling around Saint-Côme-du-Mont in search of his stick. Out of desperation, he got rid of his SCR 300 radio and came across a transformer that he destroyed with TNT. The day of June 6 was spent waiting, with Joe hiding in a hedge. The next day he was captured as he was dozing in a ditch. Joe then went through one of the most terrible experiences of his life. The Germans stuck him in an orchard north of Saint-Côme-du-Mont along with dozens of other paratroopers. This orchard was lined with tall trees and a trooper hung there, dangling miserably by the lines of his parachute. Joe said that all day on June 7, the German troops (many of whom were *Ost Truppen*) passing on the road that bordered the field, took pot shots at the body of this para, to the point of deforming it and practically removing his head! This trooper was none other than Joe's CO, Lt Colonel Robert Wolverton, killed before reaching the ground of Normandy....

Joe's odyssey was only just beginning. On the evening of June 7, the Germans escorted the long line of prisoners towards Carentan. Joe was led into a bunker held by *FJ-Regt. 6.* paratroopers. They took his clothes and even his dog tags. The following scene seems quite unreal; Joe was brought to an officer for questioning. At the side of this officer, stood a young woman that Joe knew! The woman spoke to him in perfect English and talked about England, pubs where they had gone together, paras of his platoon whose names she knew and who were, according to her, already dead... Joe was devastated; they tried to extract the radio codes from him. Even worse, Joe thought the woman knew that he had carried out missions with the Resistance. Joe understood and spoke German, but he did not want that fact to be known. He resisted and gave only "name, rank, serial number". In a long line, the prisoners marched along the N13 main highway towards Carentan. Allied aircraft controlled the sky. The P47s strafed everything that moved and the column of prisoners came under attack. Joe took the opportunity to escape. For two days, he hid in the marshes around Carentan to try to escape being found by the omnipresent Germans. Weary, he was soon recaptured and was taken by night in a truck to "Starvation Hill", the courtyard of a stud farm at St Lô where a hundred starving paras were gathered. There were more interrogations. Joe resisted, Joe rebelled, swore, insulted, spat... the butt of a Mauser put him into a coma. Then came the next incredible episode. Joe was in a hospital in Paris. He got out of bed and in the company of a thousand American, and also British prisoners, he was paraded through the streets of Paris and was insulted and spat on by a hateful crowd of Parisians! From the Gare de l'Est, he embarked in a cattle wagon towards Germany, then to a Stalag in Poland.

Joe dreamed only of escaping again and he made three attempts. One of his attempts took him to Berlin that was being bombed day and night by the Allies. Then came another horrific episode; Joe was alone, hungry and cold, in a bombed marshaling yard. He revealed himself to a civilian who led him to a cellar promising him help.

WESTERN UNION

Z148 46 GOVT=WUX WASHINGTON DC 8 153P

WILLIAM BEYRLE=

1451 FRANKLIN ST MK=

THE SECRETARY OF WAR ASKS THAT I ASSURE YOU OF HIS DEEP SYMPATHY IN THE LOSS OF YOUR SON TECHNICIAN FOURTH GRADE JOSEPH R BEYRLE WHO WAS PREVIOUSLY REPORTED CAPTURED CORRECTED REPORT NOW RECEIVED STATES HE WAS KILLED IN ACTION TEN JUNE IN FRANCE LETTER FOLLOWS=

J A ULIO THE ADJUTANT GENERAL.

Telegram informing Joe's parents of his death in combat.

Joseph Beyrle was a seasoned parachutist, nicknamed "Jumping Joe" because he would not miss a jump. His adventures would make a perfect Hollywood story. Joe landed on the roof of the Saint-Côme-du-Mont church and he could have become the John Steele of the 101st Airborne.

821 aircraft (as well as the C-47 planes of the 52nd TCW added at the last moment for Ridgway) to which were added 20 Pathfinder sticks, of the IW Troop Carrier Command, were used to drop 13,348 paratroopers of the 82nd and 101st Airborne Divisions. 6,928 men and 443 C-47s, Mission Albany for the 101st Airborne Division. Three did not take off and 21 were lost with 196 damaged. 512 gilders were released (220 Horsas and 292 Wacos), notably transporting 281 Jeeps. Five did not take off and seven were shot down.

Joe was in plain clothes and unarmed. Gestapo brutes burst in and Joe was taken away and beaten again in a cellar. The Gestapo wanted to shoot him as a spy. He only owed his salvation to the unexpected intervention of a *Luftwaffe* officer who convinced them that his American paratrooper story was true. He found himself back in the stalag in Poland. It was now February, 1945. One morning, the guards got up and left and Joe went on the run. He wandered over snow-covered Polish plains. Hunger brought him to an apparently disused farm. To his horror, the whole family was in the yard... machine-gunned. He heard the noise of tanks; it was the Red Army! Quickly, Joe approached the commander of the tank troop, who was a woman. She accepted that he join them. For several weeks, Joe lived the daily life of a Russian tank troop where he saw their often vodka-soaked courage and their cruelty towards the hated enemy, and the political commissars who encouraged the most desperate acts... as far as the Elbe. Joe was wounded by shrapnel and experienced a further crazy episode. He was taken to a hospital in the ruins of Warsaw. Conditions there were appalling and it was a place only fit for dying in. Marshal Zhukov himself arrived. He wanted to meet the "American". He issued him with a pass. Joe left the hospice and was welcomed by sisters of a Polish Catholic order. They put him back on his feet and Joe decided to go to Moscow and to the American Embassy. His pass was pure gold. Wherever he went Zhukov's signature opened doors. By train, car and truck, he reached Moscow. He knocked at the US embassy door where he told his story. He was treated, but the next day, embassy agents, escorted by Marines came to question him. He understood that they took him for a spy. The "real" Joe Beyrle, had been killed on June 6 in Normandy. His body, with his dog tags, had been found and been buried at Muskegon where a religious service had been held. His parents had already received $ 10,000 insurance compensation. Joe understood that a German must have put on his clothes and tried to escape, and then his body was found. They took his fingerprints to compare them. Washington's answer took several days to arrive and the Marines, convinced of his imposture, did not go easily on him! Finally the truth came out. Joe was able to go home via Odessa. He was reunited with his parents at the beginning of May 45. "The Simple Sound of Freedom" - Thomas H. Taylor

Joe's POW mug shot that was taken by the Germans upon his arrival at the Stalag.

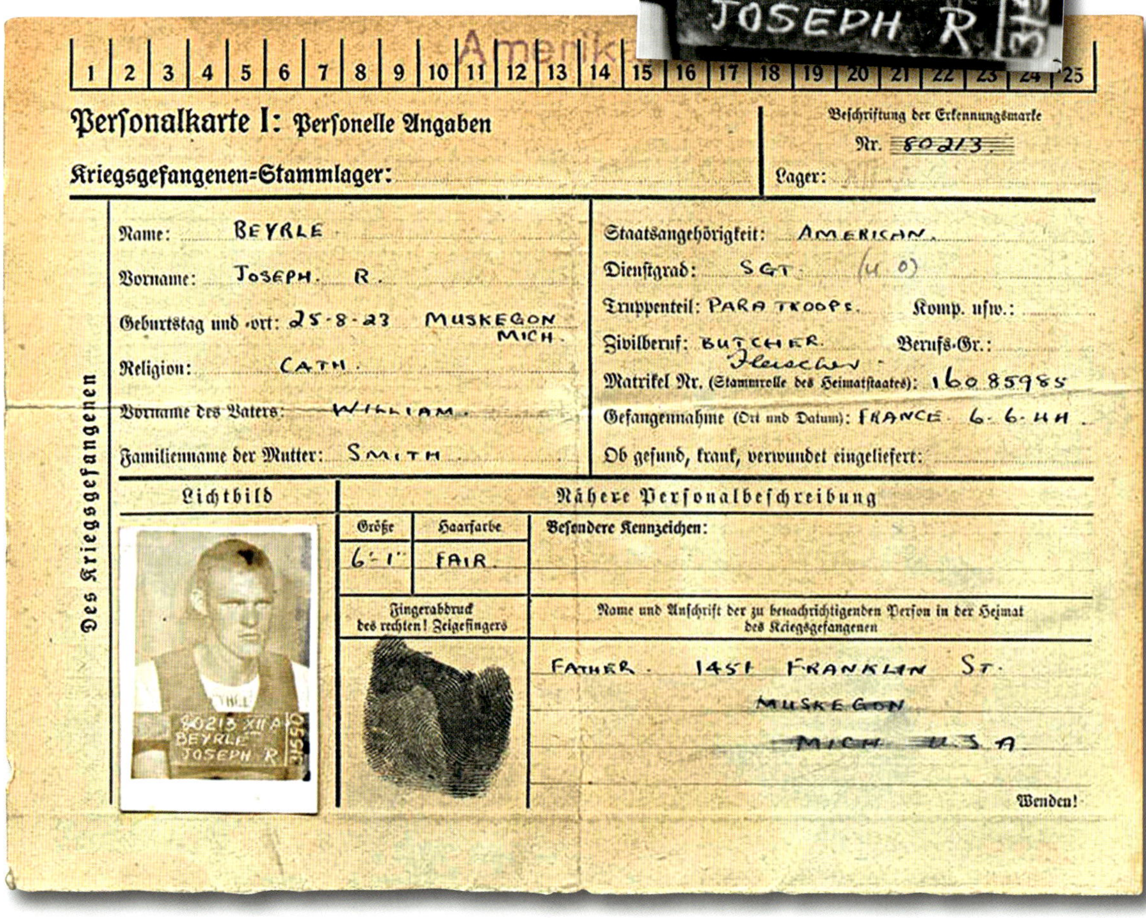

1 | 2 | 3 | 4 | 5 | 6 | 7 | 8 | 9 | 10 | 11 | 12 | 13 | 14 | 15 | 16 | 17 | 18 | 19 | 20 | 21 | 22 | 23 | 24 | 25

Amerik...

Personalkarte I: Personelle Angaben

Kriegsgefangenen-Stammlager:

Beschriftung der Erkennungsmarke
Nr. 80213
Lager:

Des Kriegsgefangenen

Name: BEYRLE
Vorname: JOSEPH R.
Geburtstag und -ort: 25-8-23 MUSKEGON MICH.
Religion: CATH.
Vorname des Vaters: WILLIAM.
Familienname der Mutter: SMITH

Staatsangehörigkeit: AMERICAN.
Dienstgrad: SGT. (U O)
Truppenteil: PARA TROOPS. Komp. usw.:
Zivilberuf: BUTCHER. Fleischer. Berufs-Gr.:
Matrikel Nr. (Stammrolle des Heimatstaates): 16085985
Gefangennahme (Ort und Datum): FRANCE. 6-6-44.
Ob gesund, krank, verwundet eingeliefert:

Lichtbild

Nähere Personalbeschreibung

Größe	Haarfarbe	Besondere Kennzeichen:
6'1"	FAIR	

Fingerabdruck des rechten! Zeigefingers

Name und Anschrift der zu benachrichtigenden Person in der Heimat des Kriegsgefangenen

FATHER. 1451 FRANKLIN ST.
MUSKEGON
MICH. U.S.A.

Wenden!

Captain Harold E. van Antwerp; the cursed dagger!

The third battalion of the 506th PIR was literally decapitated in the first minutes of the invasion. Its leaders, Bob Wolverton and George Grant, had not even set foot on Norman soil as they killed in their harnesses north of Saint-Côme-du-Mont. As early as 6 June, other company commanders, staff officers or platoon leaders suffered the same fate, Mc Knight, Chambliss, Howard, Machen... others were wounded or taken prisoner.

Captain Harold E. van Antwerp was commander of G Company from Toccoa. He was also killed a few minutes after jumping into Normandy. There is a legend concerning his death which stems from his body having been seen hanging in a barn, still in his harness, his stomach opened up by his own English commando dagger that he had bought in England. The report of the Grave Registration (the unit responsible for collecting and burying the bodies on battlefields) indicates that, among the wounds observed on his body, was a bullet in his head and multiple abdominal lacerations; something which backs up the legend!

This same Fairbairn-type dagger engraved with his name was found in Holland a few months later on a German prisoner. Paratroopers executed him, having noticed the name of its original owner.

Lt Col. Joel Lee Crouch, "Joe" or "Colonel Joe", pathfinder pilot

Born in Minnesota on 22 November 1910, Joel Lee Crouch was the headmaster of a middle school in Hannah, North Dakota.

He got his flying license in 1933 and, from April 1935 to May 1942, worked as a commercial pilot for United Airlines. He was then called up along with 96 other commercial pilots who were to form the foundations of the Troop Carriers. Wings Operation Officer of the 52nd Troop Carrier Wing in North Africa in the summer of 1943, he became one of the most ardent advocates of the pathfinders idea, scouts who would be tasked with marking out drop zones before the main force arrived. He played a decisive role in the creation of the pathfinders school at North Witham in England in April 1944 and became the first and only Commanding Officer of the IX TCC Pathfinder Group.

Some of the operational uses of the Pathfinders were applied for the 505th and 504th PIR jumps at Salerno (Italy) in September 1943. However, it was in England, early 1944, that Crouch really put into place his ideas with the creation of the Pathfinder School, made up of volunteer pilots from the three Troop Carrier Wings, and volunteers from the 101st and 82nd Airborne Divisions. Crouch gathered his volunteers at North Witham and said to them: *"I don't know where we're going, nor when we're going, no more than what we'll do when we get there; but I promise you one thing, we should have fun...You are free to refuse."* Not one man changed his mind. Crouch had the particularity of having flown lead planes in the following operations: Husky (Sicily, July 1943), Avalanche (Salerno, September 1943). He led the way during Operation Neptune, the jump into Normandy on 6 June, 1944, dropping the first Pathfinders of the 377th PFAB and 502nd PIR of Captain Frank Lillyman, over Saint-Germain-de-Varreville. His C-47 bore N° 42-93098 of the 94th TCS, 439th TCG, 9th AF USAAF. Serial #1 Chalk #1 Copilot, Capt. Vito S. Pedone, Capt. William Culp (navigator) - Capt. Edward E. Cannon (navigator) - Cpl. Harold E. Conrad (radio-operator. He passed away on 16 August 1997.

Captain Harold van Antwerp on the firing range at Clemson instructing Private Wilbur D. Croteau, G company 506th PIR. Croteau jumped on D-Day as a pathfinder in plane chalk N°9. He was killed in action on 9 June...

Below, left: At North Witham airfield, Lt. Colonel Joel Crouch and his crew, Cpl. Harold E. Conrad, radio operator, Capt. Edward E. Cannon, Capt. William Culp, navigator, Capt. Vito S. Pedone, co-pilot, Lt. Col. Joel L. Crouch, pilot, in front of their C-47, #42-93098. This was the leading plane of the IX Troop Carrier Pathfinder Group and it would be the first aircraft over the Normandy Drop zones, dropping 101st Airborne Pathfinders. Crouch took off at 21:54 hours on 5 June 1944.

Below: Colonel Joel Crouch, pathfinder pioneer, always in the leading plane, in Normandy, Holland or Germany...

2. Securing Access to Utah Beach

The 101st Airborne missions for D-Day were as follows: Capture and hold the four causeways from Utah. Destroy the heavy battery of St Martin-de-Varreville and the gunners' billets in Mezieres. To seize the lock at Barquette, to destroy all the bridges over the Douve river and hold a defensive line in order to protect the southern flank of the Landings.

Virgil Danforth; Sniper's duel in Pouppeville

Corporal Virgil Danforth, a G/501st "boy" from Indianapolis, jumped into Normandy on June 6 with a .03 Springfield rifle. He was the first to enter Pouppeville, shooting no less than 9 Germans with a bullet in the head as they poked out from ditches, where the enemy defenders tried to protect themselves. The story goes that John Boitano B/506th was to go to Pouppeville June 6, but did not succeed until the next day. He noticed that the dead Germans he found all seemed to have been shot in the head, probably victims of Danforth's skill. Danforth thus became one of the 25 members of the 501st PIR to receive a DSC. Private Meryl Tinkleberg, also of G/501st PIR, cleared out a machine-gun nest in Pouppeville and killed its squad. The Germans were holed up in the big house east of the village. Virgil tried to draw their attention in order to allow Medic T/5 Harold Nolicy rescue a wounded sergeant. A bullet hit his helmet and split in two, with one half hitting his head.

Pouppeville, was the the junction between the men of the 4th Infantry Division who had landed at Utah, and the Paratroopers of the 101st. It saw both American and German snipers show their skill, at times dramatically. Thus, Private Henry Gullick of HQ 3/501st, was killed on approaching the village. Not far from him, Lieutenant Nathan M. Marks, of G Company was also shot down. Joe "Jesse" C. Garcia came face to face with a German and this confrontation cost him his life. Medic Edwin S. Hohl and Earle F. Williams were also hit by sniper fire. Among those wounded were James F. Hubard and Corporal Vernon Kraeger.

Below, right: Virgil Danforth, the American soldier of WWII was very much like Virgil Danforth, raised in the hardships of the Great Depression, capable of adapting to all situations in the field and excelling in the art of rifle shooting. (Mark Bando)

Below: The 1903 Springfield rifle was in use in the US Army at the outbreak of WWII and would soon be replaced by the M1 Garand. Most marksmen, however, still retained a liking for the 1903... (US Army)

Harrison C. Summers, Sergeant York of the 101st Airborne

Harrison C. Summers was born on July 12, 1918 in the small village of Catawba, West Virginia. He worked before the war as a miner in Rivesville before joining the army. He was a Staff Sergeant with the 1st Battalion, 502nd PIR, 101st Airborne. He distinguished himself in Normandy on June 6, 1944 when taking Objective WXYZ, the hamlet of Mezières near Saint-Germain-de-Varreville, of which the real name was unknown to the intelligence services.

The 1st battalion of the 502nd PIR, commanded by Patrick Cassidy, was tasked with securing the northern flank of the invasion in the Utah Beach area. He had to ensure the opening of road N ° 4 for the troops that had landed at the beach, leading from Ravenoville beach, but also the neutralization of the troops billeted in the hamlet of Mézières. These German soldiers were the personnel for the guns of the nearby Saint-Martin-de-Varreville battery. The US paras were unaware that the battery's 122-mm guns had been removed by the Germans following the intense aerial bombardment in late May. However, the battery personnel, comprising of more than a hundred soldiers, had to be neutralized. Pat Cassidy ordered Summers to take around fifteen men to clear the village. Starting at 9 am on 6 June, the attack was launched from the north and west of the village.

Summers, armed with a Thompson sub-machine gun, rushed in, thinking he was followed by his fifteen soldiers. He shot the three German soldiers who had taken refuge in the first house. Private William A. Burt set up his machine-gun in front of house No. 3 and fired at the doors and windows. Lieutenant Elmer F. Brandenberger (Baker Company 502nd) decided to follow him but was wounded by a grenade explosion during the attack on the second house and was put out of action. Summers charged on the house alone and gunned down six the occupants with one machine-gun burst.

Before the attack on the next house, a captain of the 82nd Airborne joined them, accompanied by 2nd class John Camien, but he was hit within 20 yards of Summers by a sniper. His final fate and identity remain a mystery today.

Summers and Camien advanced from house to house. While one was covering, the other pushed open doors. The two men cleaned out the last five billets without taking any prisoners. The village ended with a large building. The Germans had installed a canteen there. Summers burst in on fifteen men sitting at tables and who seemed unaware of the fighting raging by their windows. They were all gunned down by the American sergeant. After leaving by the back of the building, Summers was hit by an enemy sniper, with the shots coming from a barn at the end of a field.

The barn was near a bunker filled with Germans. American fire blew up an ammunition dump and thirty Germans were killed. Shortly after, Lieutenant Colonel Patrick Cassidy and Sergeant Nickrent from Chicago, armed with his bazooka, arrived at the scene. Nickrent fired twice on the barn and set fire to the upper storey. According to George Koskimaki, it was Private Bill Burt who set off the fire by firing tracer bullets with his machine-gun.

All these actions had lasted more than 5 hours. When it was all over, Summers sat by the side of the road and lit a cigarette, feeling unwell. There were more than 30 German dead, all victims of Summers' Thompson. Thirty were taken prisoner.

For his actions in Normandy, Summers was promoted to lieutenant and recommended for the Congressional Medal of Honor. He only received the Distinguished Service Cross. He also took part in the Cole Charge on the Ingouf farm. In July 1944, he received a battlefield promotion to the rank of 2nd Lieutenant and was attached to H Company of the 502nd PIR. He was seriously wounded in Bastogne in January 1945 and sent back to the United States where he died of lung cancer in 1983. His friends are still fighting today for him to be posthumously awarded the Congressional Medal of Honor.

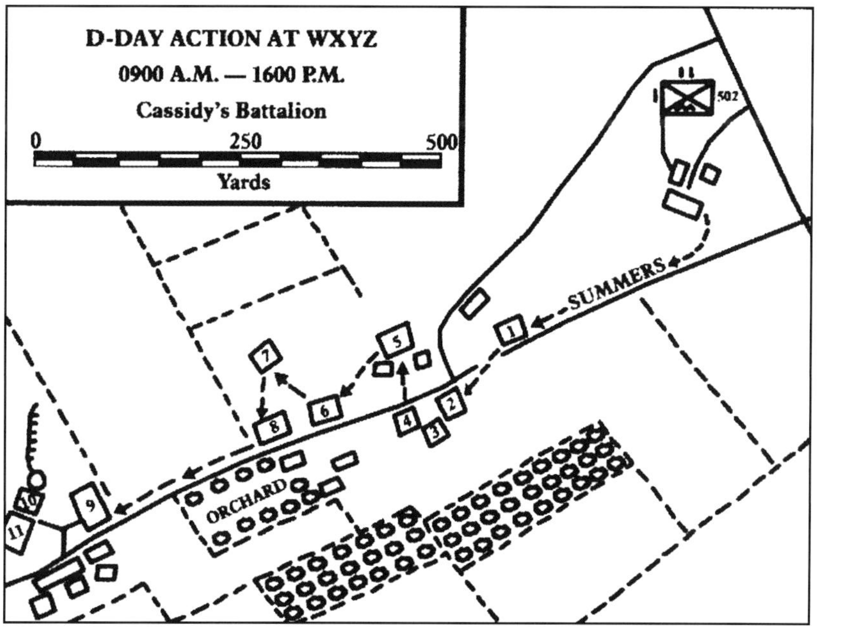

The route taken by Sgt. Harrison Summers in Mézières, at Objective WXYZ, as it was named by American planners. Most of the personnel of the Saint-Germain-de-Varreville artillery battery were billeted in the village. The guns had been removed by the end of May 1944 after severe RAF bombing raids. (Mark Bando)

Harrison Summers, the Sergeant York of the 101st.

Captain Bill Osborne (CO D/501), The ordinary fate of a D-Day Para on day 1

When Captain Bill Osborne, Commanding Officer, Dog Company 501 PIR, jumped from his C-47 on the night of June 6, 1944, his parachute suffered a roman candle and he fell like a stone over Normandy. However, a tree cushioned his fall. He was knocked out when he hit the ground, not coming round till sunrise. Semi-conscious, he saw the tip of a boot in front of his face. He wondered who could be lying next to him and gradually realized that it was... his own foot. His leg, broken in the fall, was at such an angle that he struggled to realize that it was his own foot he was looking at....

He was near the church of Angoville-au-Plain. He had kept his Thompson SMG with him, which he used to keep the Germans who were swarming over the area at bay. A MG 42 machine gun took position not far from him. With his back to a hedge, Osborne knew that the men of Colonel Ballard's 2nd Battalion were in the adjacent field, but every time a para tried to help him, he drew the fire of the MG 42. Before long, the Germans used him as bait, letting paras approach the wounded captain before gunning them down. It was only at night that Osborne was finally rescued by Dan D. Rees and Tommy Coyne of F/501 who hoisted him over the hedge... He never recovered from his broken leg and he left the army.

Major Lawrence Legere, Assistant S-3 101st Airborne; No immunity for Medics...

Lawrence Joseph Legere was born on January 2, 1919 in Leominster, Massachusetts. He graduated from West Point in 1940 and chose the paratroops. He began his career as Assistant S-3 of the 502nd Parachute Infantry. In June 1943, he became Assistant G-3 of the 101st Airborne, with the rank of Major. On June 6, he was jumpmaster, a kind of jump supervisor, in Max Taylor's plane. Legere soon found his General and many members of his headquarters on the ground. No one, however, knew their exact position. Legere went on reconnaissance with Virgil Danforth. They entered a farm occupied by an old and completely terrified couple, who showed them their position on the map and offered them bread and wine. Sure of his position, but without news of his battalions, Max Taylor decided to lead a mix of 501st and 101st officers (Higgins, Ewell, Legere, McAuliffe (2 generals and 1 colonel) and Pappas of the 326th AEB (KIA June 15)...) and some 3/501st troopers towards the objective of Pouppeville, near Causeway No. 1. The Pouppeville road was identified as Causeway No. 1, one of four routes to Utah Beach that the 101st had to secure. The small hamlet was held by Germans from the *91. Luftlande-Division* and, according to historian Mark Bando, Georgians, as well as *Grenadier- Regiment 1058*, according to S.L.A. Marshall.

The 4th ID landed at Utah Beach at 6:30. By noon, the first tanks were at Pouppeville. Ewell and his 3/501 boys cleaned out the

Before D-Day, Bill Osborne was with the 501st where they had been billeted in a tented camp on Lady Craven's estate since January 1944, at Hampstead Marshall, near Ramsbury. (Mark Bando)

village house by house. Major Larry Legere was hiding in a ditch. He rushed across the road when a shot rang out. He was hit in the thigh by a wooden bullet. The bullet went through his shovel, then his knee and came out through his thigh. Legere screamed with pain. Medic T/5 Edwin Hohl, a kid from Buffalo, New York, rushed over and, while giving him first aid, was shot dead by a sniper with a bullet in his chest. Lifeless, he slumped onto Legere's body. Larry Legere insists that the red crosses on Eddie Hohl's helmet and armband were clearly visible. (1)

Coming up behind Colonel Julian Ewell, the men of G/501st led the assault and from 9am, seized Pouppeville by encircling it and by engaging in house-to-house fighting. The German CP in town was reached at 11am and 38 Germans surrendered after the paratroopers opened bazooka fire. They lost 25 men whereas 6 troopers were killed and 12 were wounded. The link up with the 8th IR soldiers from Captain George Mabry's 8th Inf.Rgt. Soldiers of the 4th ID was completed shortly after 11am.

Legere was evacuated to Utah Beach in the afternoon. He remained in the army, and served in Korea, France and Washington with President Kennedy as defense advisor.

(1) There were also many cases of German medical columns being strafed by allied aircraft – such is the cruelty of war... (Publisher's note)

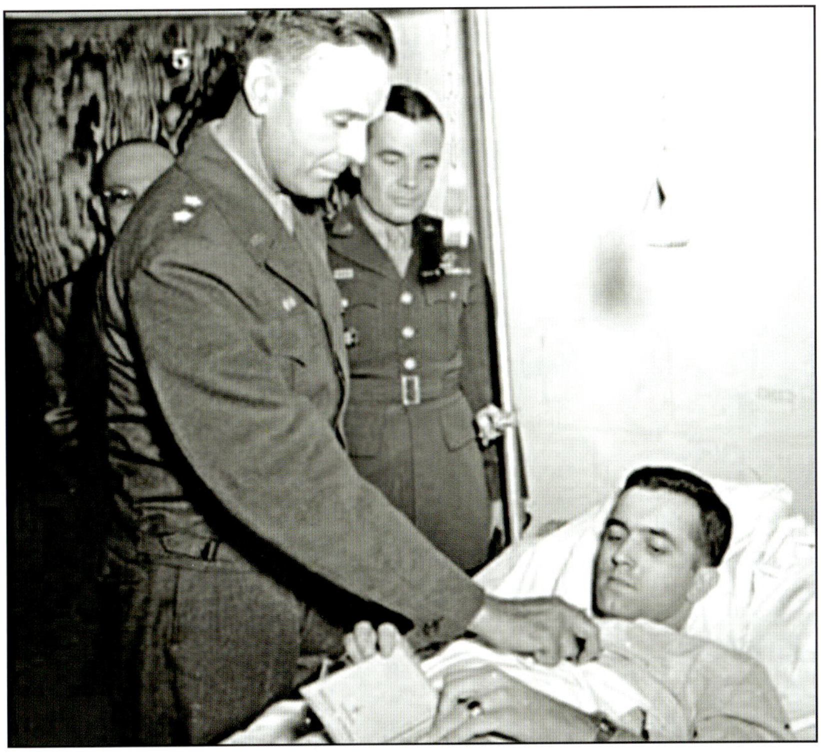

He was recovering in an English hospital when Max Taylor and Anthony McAuliffe awarded him his DSC. (US Army)

Below: Larry Legere, staff officer; his first combat experience would turn out to be a painful one when he was seriously wounded by snipers in Pouppeville. (Michael Legere)

Opposite: by sundown on 6 June, the positions held by the 101st regiments were as follows; all causeways to the beach, from Ravenoville to the north, to Pouppeville in the south had been secured. But the Americans had failed to secure or destroy the southern bridges over the Douve river. The German paratroopers of *F.J.-Regt. 6* were blocking Taylor's moves. To the west of the Merderet, the 82nd Airborne regiments, the 507th and 508th were in a similar situation.

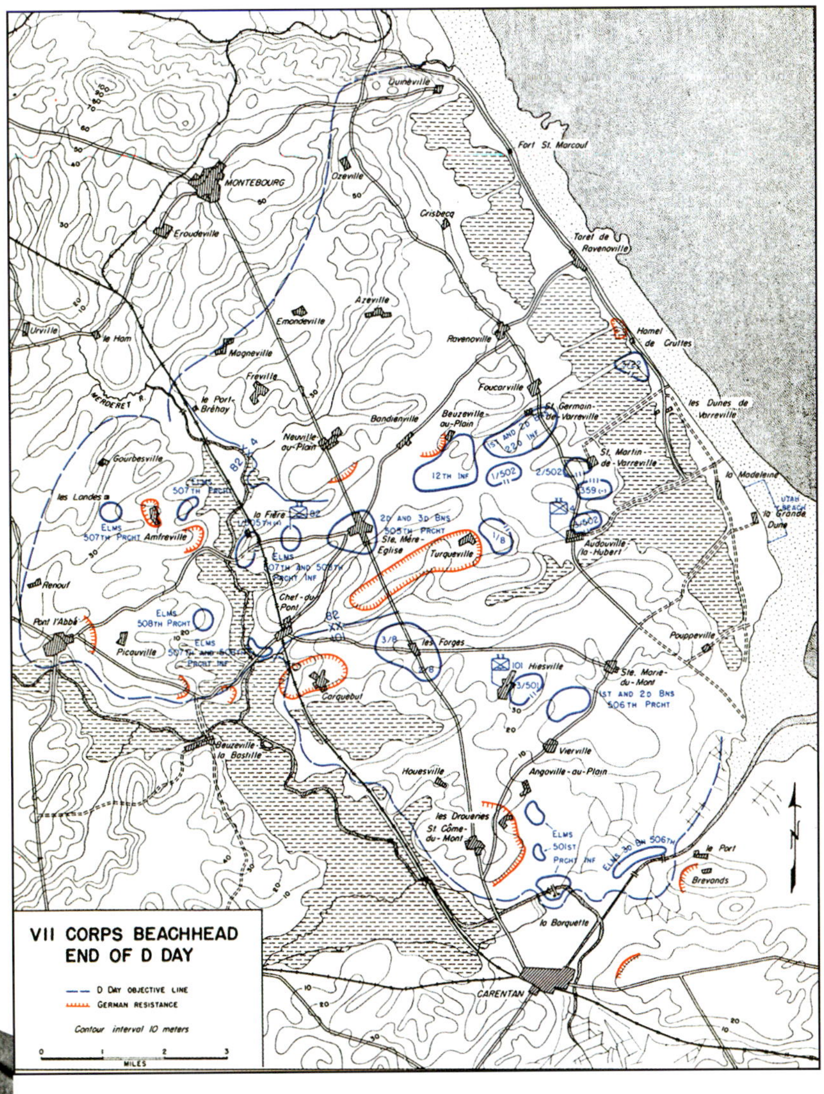

3. The Geronimos at Carentan

Below: Colonel Johnson's cadres at Fort Benning during parachute training. From left to right, Carrel, Robert Ballard, Red Shelby, Robert Carroll, Julian Ewell and Howard Johnson. (US Army)

Colonel Howard Ravenscroft Johnson's 501st PIR, the first paratrooper regiment formed from scratch in February 1942 in Toccoa, took off from Merryfield and Welton airfields on June 6, 1944. It had a strength of 2,175 men and 168 officers. His Regimental Headquarters (commanded by Captain William G. Burd) and the First Battalion of Lt Colonel Robert C. Carrol, had to seize the locks of La Barquette on the Douve river. Lt. Harold Young, of Charley Company, 326th Airborne Engineer Battalion was to blow up the bridge over the Douve, but he never reached his objective.

Lt Colonel Robert Ballard's Second Battalion was to destroy bridge N ° 2 on the river Douve and seize St-Côme-du-Mont. The Third Battalion led by Lt Colonel Julian J. Ewell was to land on Drop Zone "C" and provide security for the headquarters of the 101st Airborne in Hiesville.

In spite of the bad drops and scattering of the units, most of these objectives were achieved as of June 6th, except for the missions of the 2/501st that was blocked in its attempt to approach St-Côme-du-Mont in the sector Droueries-Basse and Haute-Addeville.

The most important battle of the 501st was fought near Pénême, at an intersection now called "Hell's Corner". A force of about 150 paratroopers commanded by Johnson himself, wiped out the entire first battalion of Fallschirmjäger Regiment 6. *commanded by* Hauptmann *Emil Preikschat. Johnson received the Silver Star for this military exploit.*

Above: on activation of the 501st Parachute Infantry Regiment early 1942, its commanding officer, Howard Johnson, asked Sergeants Richard Clarke, Lee Clayman and Eugen Amburgey to come up with a regimental insignia. They designed an Indian head with a flash and parachute canopy. But the Department of Heraldry ruled it out, arguing that the 501st Battalion already had its insignia. Johnson could not care less and went ahead with the design of his liking, making pocket patches worn stateside and after VE-Day in Europe. (Private collection.)

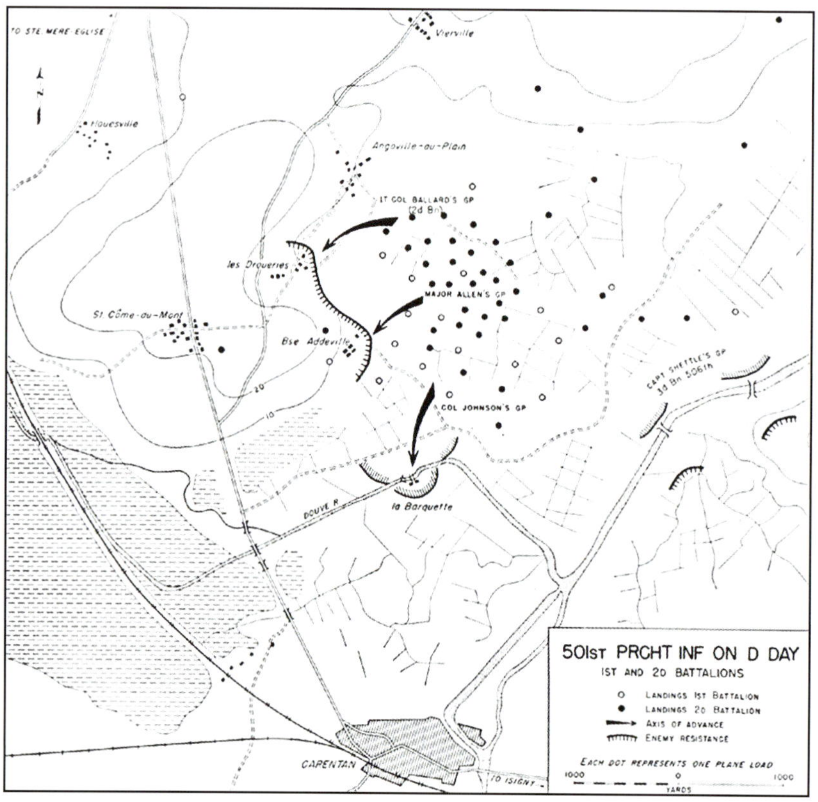

Opposite: the taking of the La Barquette locks was a relatively easy business, but moving on Saint-Côme-du-Mont was slow and took two days of heavy fighting around Les Droueries and Basse Addeville. The Douve river bridges on the main RN13 highway could not even be approached by Johnson's men.

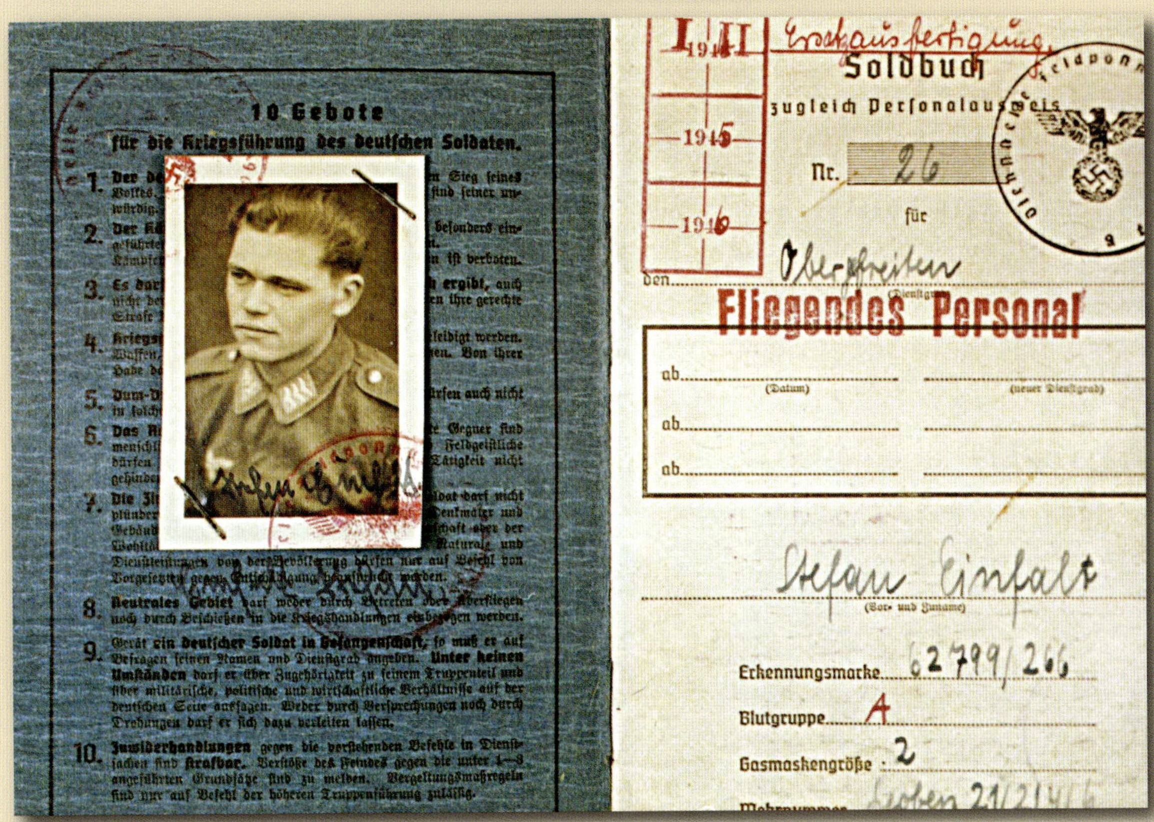

Above: German paratrooper's helmet, similar to those used by *F.J. Reg. 6* (Private collection.)

Opposite: Soldbuch (soldiers ID and paybook) belonging to *Obergefreiter* Stefan Einhalt of *F.J. Reg.6* which was wiped out at Hell's Corner. This soldier was one of the many German paratroopers ambushed by Johnson's men. It was taken from the body of the dead soldier by Harold Paulson of C/501st) (Mark Bando)

Dog tags belonging to Sergeant Thomas Rice, C/501st. (Thomas Rice)

A night at La Barquette, Thomas M. Rice

Sergeant Thomas M. Rice took off from Merryfield on June 5, 1944, as jumpmaster of his 2nd platoon stick, mortar section, C Company 501st PIR. First to jump on DZ "D", he was surprised by the excessive speed of his C-47, and remained hanging onto the door, his body hanging outside the cabin. He managed to free himself and landed with his buddies, Frank Figarotta and Tony Das, both with the mortar platoon, north of Addeville. While trying to cross a canal, Das almost drowned and the base of the mortar sank to the bottom of the water. Rice and Figarotta decided to throw the rest of the mortar, barrel and tripod into the canal. Quickly joined by other troopers, Rice located his position and joined Major J. Allen, S-3 of the 501st. Whilst passing through Basse Addeville, Figarotta was shot in the head. Rice and Allen's men joined Johnson at La Barquette. About 40 men from different units, commanded by Lt Lee J. Bowers, reached the locks under German sniper and mortar fire. Supply Sergeant Lawrence Ardrey was killed by a sniper 100 meters north of the lock, while Pvt Milario Campos, the first to reach the other bank, was wounded by a mortar projectile that blinded him in one eye and broke one of his arms.

On the evening of June 7, Rice, along with Tony Das and George Zeberowski, was sent across the Barquette lock to search the Parey farm on the south bank of the river Douve. The three men found Claude Parey's house deserted. They set up their advanced position in the garden facing Carentan, by the river. They had an excellent open field of fire in front of them. They dug their foxholes on the edge of the embankment bordering the garden and set up an alarm system at a distance of 50 meters from their position, by using poles connected together by parachute lines from which they hung food cans filled with nails or pebbles. They then took up position in their foxholes, and stayed connected to each other with parachute lines attached to their wrists. At the slightest warning, they could thus alert each other by pulling on the line. Around two o'clock in the morning, a German patrol entered their alert perimeter and triggered the improvised alarm. Rice, Das and Zeberowski simultaneously fired with their two M-1s and their Thompson. Several Germans were hit and they retreated to the south. They left one of their own screaming and groaning on the floor. Throughout the rest of the night, the wounded German could be heard groaning. Rice dared not come out for fear of a trick. At the first light of day, one of the three paratroopers left his foxhole and finished off the wounded soldier with a M-3 knife. He was a thirty-year old *Fallschirmjäger*, whom the paratroopers buried at the edge of the garden, his dog tags hanging visibly on a hastily-made cross. *"It was a long and miserable night, like so many others before the war ended,"* Tom Rice wrote in his memoirs.

Above: The La Barquette locks and Paret house in the foreground where Tom Rice spent the night of 6 June. Tom was at this moment the southernmost advanced party of the 101st south of the Douve.

Opposite: Tom Rice, a few days before embarking in Marseille for his return trip to the US in 1945. (Thomas Rice)

Below: The route taken by Thomas Rice on D-Day.

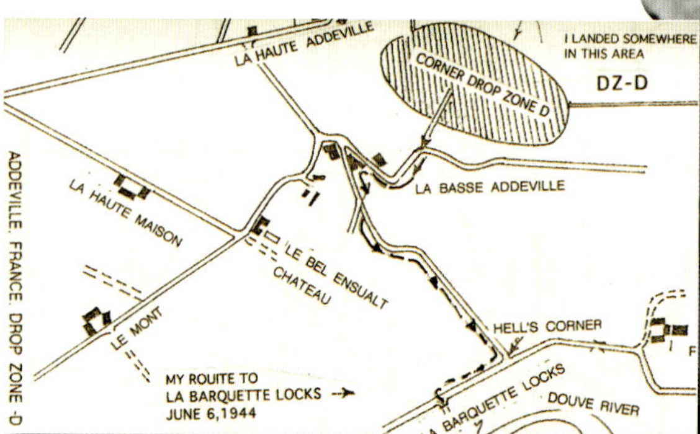

Leo Francis Runge, HQ 501st An Austrian receives the German surrender...

Leo Runge was born in Austria on August 8, 1923. His parents emigrated to Canada, then moved to the United States. He joined the US Army in order to gain US citizenship. He chose the paratroopers and ended up at the Demolition platoon of Howard Johnson's 501st HQ company.

He jumped into the courtyard of Château Bel Esnaut on June 6, and managed to escape and join the Barquette area. Along the way, he saw the bodies of Lt Colonel Carrol, commander of the 1/501st, and Lt. John Atkinson of HQ 1/501st company.

At around 3 pm on Wednesday, June 7, 1944, Colonel Howard Ravenscroft Johnson, CO of the 501st Parachute Infantry, held his main objective, the Barquette lock. From the north-east and Sainte-Marie-du-Mont, he saw a large force walking nonchalantly across the marshland. Johnson had about 250 men with him positioned on both banks of the Douve. He put around 150 troopers and 6 of his 8 .30 cal in position along the small road that leads to Pénême, an intersection that would later be named Hell's corner. The approaching force was quickly identified as that of the 1st battalion, led by *Hauptmann* Emil Preikschat, of *Fallschirmjäger Regiment 6.* commanded by *Major* Friedrich August Baron von Heydte. At 4 pm, while the Germans were only 300 meters away, Johnson opened fire. The Germans went to ground in the tall grass of the marshes, hid in canals and ditches and suffered heavy losses. They fired a flare that drew mortar fire on the Americans from St-Côme-du-Mont and Carentan. After 30 minutes of intensive firing, Johnson knew he held the Germans at his mercy. But he knew, above all, that he was dangerously short of ammunition. At 6:30 that morning, the US Air Corps had tried to resupply them but the bundles had fallen into German hands, and not a single bullet could be recovered. The *Fallschirmjäger* numbered 500. If they realized how short the troopers were on ammo, they alone could outflank Johnson. It was then that the first cries of "*Kamerad*" resounded in the swamps. More and more Germans seemed to want to surrender. Johnson then decided to negotiate the total surrender of the *Fallschirmjäger*. He took two soldiers to serve as escort and interpreter. This is where the story and the testimonies diverge.

Lieutenants Rapport and Northwood, the official para-historians of the 101st, named Pvt Leo Fran-

Above: Hell's Corner is the intersection above the La Barquette locks.

Left: Leo Runge, before fighting with distinction at Hell's Corner, Leo fought at Château Bel Esnaut. He jumped out of Colonel Johnson's plane and landed on top of the château, which he then "visited", pistol in hand, killing a few German soldiers and officers before making his way to La Barquette. (Mark Bando)

Below: Hell's Corner after the fighting... (US Army)

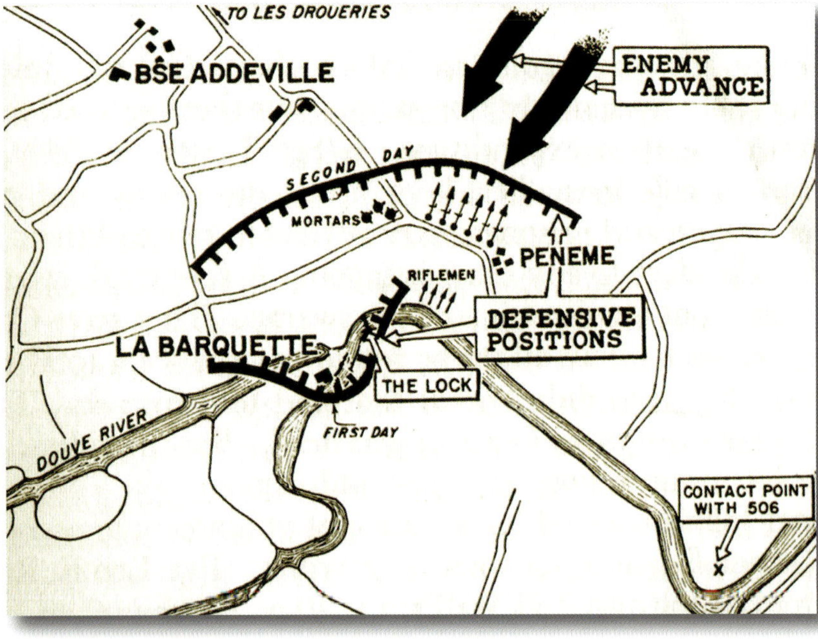

The battle of Hell's Corner: some 150 US paratroopers ambushed over 500 German *Fallschirmjäger*. Only 26 of the latter made it back to Carentan.

cis Runge, demo platoon RHQ 501 and T5 William F Lenz as being these men, whereas William Critchell, 501st Trooper and author of the history of the 501st, named Pvt Robert Nicolai and Norman Blanchette. Recently Birdlegs Dickson of C/326th Abn Engineer Bn said he accompanied Johnson in his attempts to parlay (It is said to be his helmet at the Dead Man's Corner museum).

Hauptmann Emil Preikschat commanded 1st battalion, F.J. Reg. 6 at Hell's Corner. He was posted as missing there.

So was it Runge-Lenz or Nicolai-Blanchette? It seems, in fact, that Johnson made two attempts to parlay. The first, with Runge and Lenz was aborted, while the 3 men advanced towards the Germans with an orange flag attached to Runge's rifle, the Germans stopped shooting, but not the Americans, to the fury of Johnson who ordered the ceasefire. The *FJ*s remained hidden, then opened fire again. Runge's arm and Johnson's hand were both hit. The shooting resumed and the three negotiators crawled back to the American lines. 30 minutes later, the shooting lessened in intensity and shouts of "*Kamerad*" were again heard. A German approached, explaining that his comrades wanted to surrender, but that their officers threatened to shoot them. Runge picked up a white sheet from a farm in Pénême, gave it to the wounded German and told him to return to his officers to inform them that they had 30 minutes to throw down helmets and rifles, and to raise their hands up to US forces. The Germans left, and the shooting resumed. 30 minutes later, many Germans, disarmed and without helmets, began to get up, but there were shots from US lines. Close to Johnson, Lieutenant Owens was taking pot shots at the Germans who had surrendered. Johnson kicked his butt so hard that Owens finished up in the mud.

From 6 pm and during the next 3 hours, a long column of German prisoners left the marshes, heading for Pénême. 150 *FJ* had been killed, 350 were captured, 25 are said to have reached Carentan... Johnson counted 10 killed and 33 wounded. The German officer commanding 1st battalion of *FJ Reg. 6.*, *Hauptmann* Emil Preikschat stepped forward. He refused to be disarmed, appealed to the Geneva Convention and claimed to want to negotiate... Johnson pushed him into the column of prisoners with a shrug.

The last act of this day of June 7th took place while the long column of German prisoners was on the small road to Pénême, an 88 shell fired from Carentan fell on the road, killing some 20 Germans, as well as the Regimental adjutant of 501 PIR, Captain Altus Mc Reynolds.

Runge later received the DSC for his actions on June 7.

Saint-Côme-du-Mont was finally taken on June 8, after the German paratroopers' hold on the 2/501st was loosened by the intervention of the big guns of the Navy (USS Quincy) firing from the open sea.

On June 9, the 501st regrouped near Vierville, crossed the Douve at Brévands on the 10th, joined Catz and prepared to encircle Carentan by Saint-Hilaire-Petitville.

On June 12, the 3/501st attacked the strongly defended Hill 30 south of Carentan with fixed bayonets.

The survivors joined up with the 506th PIR from the west. The 501st participated the next day in the terrible fighting to repel the counterattack of the *17. SS-Panzergrenadier-Division*.

The 501st later received the Presidential Unit Citation.

Robert O. Nicolai, HQ 501st: a James Bond in the 101st...

Robert O. Nicolai was from Midlothian, Illinois. He served in the Merchant Navy and would receive a Bronze Star in Normandy. According to Lawrence Critchell, author of "Four Stars of Hell", he was with Johnson during the first attempts at Hell's Corner, to negotiate with the German paratroopers of the 1st battalion of *F.J.-Regt. 6*. He later served in Holland as personal bodyguard and favorite of Howard Johnson. At the end of October 1944 he was part of the famous "Incredible Patrol", a small group of 5 scouts from the Intelligence Section HQ Company, 501st PIR that crossed the Rhine and brought back 36 prisoners at the end of an amazing expedition behind the German lines. All members of this patrol received the Silver Star, except Nicolai.

When Johnson was fatally hit by shrapnel near Heteren in the Netherlands on October 6, 1944, Nicolai was the first to be at his side. Johnson, who was suffering horribly, asked him to hit him and knock him out. When the 501st was deactivated in the summer of '45, he was transferred to A Company of the 506th PIR. While the Regiment was in Joigny, huge quantities of German weapons were stored in the camp awaiting destruction. It would appear that Nicolai built up his own stocks, to be later sold on to the Israelis.

Nicolai was an unusual character who tried out small jobs after the war, but his desire for action was stronger and, in 1948,he volunteered to be part of the crew of SS Ben Hecht. This ship was loaded with more than 700 concentration camp survivors and tried to force the British blockade to join Israel. Nicolai was stopped off Cyprus by the British, and was never heard of again...

Below: Robert Nicolai (left) was a typical Gung-Ho paratrooper. His life reads like an adventure-packed novel. He was Johnson's bodyguard and a member of "the incredible patrol" in Holland, then an arms smuggler in the Mediterranean after the war...

Top: with fixed bayonet, he stands guard and protects 501st officers Howard Johnson, Julian Ewell and Robert Ballard near Eerde in the Netherlands. (US Army)

Above: Robert Nicolai's last known picture...

Johnson at Merryfield airstrip, minutes before boarding, bound for Normandy.

"War daddy", Colonel Howard Ravenscroft Johnson, CO 501st Parachute Infantry

Rarely in the history of the US Army, let alone in the history of the US Airborne, has a commander been so strongly identified with his regiment. Howard Ravencroft Johnson fashioned, carved and chiseled his 501st Parachute Infantry in his image, his conception of what a parachute entity should be; that of all out aggression and devotion to the mission. He did not live long enough to accompany his regiment all the way to ultimate triumph, but his spirit accompanied his brave "Geronimos" to victory, and to deactivation in July 1945. Howard Johnson, nicknamed "Jumpy" for his immoderate love of jumps, "Skeets", "Old man" or "War Daddy" went to Normandy and demonstrated in the field all that the archetypal paratrooper should be in the minds of the great leaders responsible for the Airborne doctrine – James Gavin, Bill Lee or Yarborough. He was a leader from the moment he landed on Norman soil, in front of the château gate of Bel Esnaut, where he killed his first German, and his heroic action at Hell's Corner and aggressive leadership in completing the encirclement of Carentan at La Billonnerie. He was on the front line alongside his men, ready to shoot and to put his life in danger. Along with the other three 101st Airborne regiment commanders, he was decorated with the Silver Star in République square in Carentan on June 15, 1944.

Jumpy Johnson was a unique phenomenon, hailing from the heart of America to personify the courageous and brutal determination to win the war. This determination was found in each of his paratroopers. Johnson was born for a mission, World War II. He lived and fought until the war consumed him. Those who have studied the 501st know that there were no regiment commanders like him throughout the war. The life and death of Howard R Johnson were expressions of absolute conviction.

The following story unfolded as the 501st PIR occupied the grounds owned by Lady Craven at Hampstead Marshall near Newbury. George Coyne was from HQ 501st. He decided one night to go for a walk in the village with no pass. He finished his beer and when he returned to his billet, looked for a place to sneak in and avoid the sentries. A jeep appeared! It was Jumpy, driving alone, as usual. Coyne was spotted. He rushed off but Jumpy hit the accelerator. Coyne decided to cut across the fields, hoping to discourage his colonel. On the contrary, Johnson left the Jeep and started rac-

Colonel Howard R. Johnson was the epitome of the Airborne leader, a soldier with a vision of what airborne combat meant. He shaped the 501st to his image. He was "Geronimo".

ing across the English countryside. Jumpy pursued him for several kilometers, gradually gaining ground. Feeling Johnson was on his back, Coyne, out of breath, ended up throwing himself into a ditch. Also out of breath, Jumpy soon reached him. Catching his breath, the Colonel declared to his soldier that no enlisted man would EVER be able to beat him in a race. Coyne never heard of the incident again...

Johnson arrived at La Barquette at dawn on June 6 from Bel Esnaut where he landed under the nose of German sentries. He had about 150 men with him from the 1st and 2nd Battalions, as well as HQ, and some stragglers of the 506th. 200 meters from the lock, he came under mortar and 88 fire. He sent 50 men to cross the lock and occupy the south bank of the Douve. Pvt. Campos was the first to reach the other bank. He was wounded by a mortar that blinded him in one eye and broke one of his arms. The other troopers took over the lock keeper's house which was empty. They occupied some abandoned German defensive positions and found a 506th trooper with his leg torn off.

Johnson kept this small force together, protected by foxholes. Throughout the day of June 6, these troopers were copiously bombarded by German artillery from Carentan, shot at by concealed snipers and had to repulse several attempts made to infiltrate their positions.

There is some controversy at this point; Johnson left La Barquette, which he believed to be secure, to reach Major Allen and his men who were stranded at Basse Addeville. When he returned in the afternoon of the 6th with all his forces to La Barquette, it was claimed that the south of the lock had cleared off. Johnson, who was killed in Holland on October 5, could never be questioned about it.

A bell in the night...

The 2/501st PIR had trained in England to regroup after a jump, using the sound of a bronze bell and a lamp attached to the top of a stake for night jumps. Although these two devices proved to be effective in training, they were not retained for the June 6th jump. Lieutenant Ed Allworth was S-1 Battalion, Colonel Ballard's deputy. On board the C-47 which took him to Normandy, he had with him a personal equipment bundle, filled with administrative papers, notebooks and supplies necessary for his work. He added one of the bronze bells he bought at an antique store in Newbury, thinking it might be useful once on the ground. His bundle was attached to a rescue parachute, and tied to his hand by a small rope. When he jumped, the force created by the speed of the plane snapped the rope and almost tore off one of his fingers. He never found his equipment bundle. Ed was injured by grenade splinters at dawn. However, it was to him that Robert Ballard entrusted the mission to organize an aid post in Angoville-au-Plain. Ed set up the infirmary in the church, with medics Bob Wright and Kenneth Moore. Throughout the day of June 7, fighting raged around the church between the *Fallschirmjäger* and 3/506th and C/326th AEB troopers. The bell was found decades later near Tamerville farm.

2nd battalion, 501st PIR relied on a lantern attached to the top of a stick to assemble its men on D Day, as well as on a bell. Neither lantern nor bell were recovered that night. Ed Allworth was the officer who set up an aid station inside the church at Angoville-au-Plain, where medics Moore and Wright worked tirelessly for over 48 hours.

For a long time this bell was attributed to the 508th. Found near Tamerville, it could be Ed Allworth's bell that he lost during the jump on 6 June. (Private collection)

Father Sam in Blosville. (US Army)

Francis L. Sampson, 501st Infantry Parachute Chaplain, 101st Airborne, the Saint of the 501st!

Francis L. Sampson was born February 29, 1912 in Cherokee, Iowa. He studied at Notre Dame University then at St. Paul's Seminary in Minnesota where he was ordained a priest on June 1, 1941. Less than a year after his entry into the Order, in 1942, Francis L. Sampson received permission to enlist from his bishop of Des Moines. He then studied at the School of Chaplains at Harvard. Without really knowing where he was going, he volunteered for the paratroops, not thinking for one second that he might be asked to jump off a moving plane. He found himself at the Parachute School in Fort Benning at the beginning of 1943 where he followed the 4 parachutist training courses without any special favors, and came out with 5 jumps and wings. He was then sent to Camp Mackall on June 7, 1943 where the 501st Parachute Infantry Regiment was training under the command of the hard taskmaster, Howard "Jumpy" Johnson. A year later, on the night of June 6, he took off from Bedford and jumped into Normandy with the 501st, landing in a fast-flowing small river. He lost all his religious and medical material and had to dive 5 or 6 times to retrieve it. This scene appears in The Longest Day, albeit somewhat anglicized. He did not mention the Douve, but spoke of a small river with a strong current.

Perhaps it was the Douve as, when he managed to free himself from his parachute and to get to the riverbank, he saw a plane in difficulty that crashed a few hundred meters away in a large fireball. Perhaps it was the Lancaster that crashed in a place called place called "Les rats". He then reached Fortin farm where Father McGee of the 506th medics, assisted by a French family, were attending to 25 injured paratroopers. A little later, he witnessed the death of the French woman (Odette Fortin) and the young Georgette Revet, killed while going to the well for water for the wounded. He then took charge of an aid station on a farm in Basse Addeville (Photo). Germans of the *F.J.-Regt. 6* seized the farm. Two *Fallschirmjäger* troopers put him up against a wall and were about to shoot him when a young Bavarian non-commissioned officer saved his life. Sampson worked for 3 days to help the 18 wounded GIs at the farm as best he could until the return of his regiment. In the meantime, the barn was partially razed by shelling, killing two of the seriously wounded men as it collapsed. Sampson then worked as a medic at the Colombières château until the walls also collapsed here under the bombing of the *Luftwaffe*. Once his wounded were well taken care of, Sampson proposed to replace one of the exhausted doctors. Sampson went into his third night without any rest, and in the early morning, when they ran out of blood to save a wounded person, he spontaneously volunteered to give his own...

Sampson later jumped into Holland. Again, he fell... into the moat of Heeswijk Castle! He was in Bastogne in December 44 and left with his jeep on Christmas Eve on a report that there were injured GI's somewhere. He did not find the wounded men but came across a group of Germans. He ended the war in a Stalag. Sampson had not finished with war though. He accompanied the 101st in Korea and Vietnam, with the rank of Lieutenant Colonel.

Francis Sampson: the iconic figure of "Father Sam" at the Blosville temporary cemetery. It would appear that the 501st Catholic chaplain landed in the Douve river. He moved from there to the Fortin farm in Pénême and helped Father McGee set up an aid station. He then moved to Addeville where he set up another aid station. He barely escaped summary execution and moved on to Blosville, then to the Colombières château. His actions during the very first days of the invasion are legendary and, above all, superhuman. Johnson put in a request for a Medal of Honor which Taylor downgraded to a DSC as he had decided that a sole MoH could be awarded to a member of the Division throughout the entire Normandy campaign.

Rudy Korvas
Death before Dishonor

The Dirty 13 was born as early as 1943 at Camp Mackall. They were less famous than the Filthy 13, as they had not been lucky enough to have a Signal Corps team to film their boarding at Exeter on June 5 or a wide coverage in the Stars and Stripes of August 1944. This was a group of friends of the First Platoon, F/501st PIR who actually numbered 12. Eager to defy destiny, they fought under the name the of the Dirty 13. Their recognition sign was the skull and crossbones tattooed on their left forearm. When John Zeilmeier joined them, he had it tattooed on his right arm. Among these Dirty 13, we know Claude V. Williams, Oris Loudermilk (Co. HQ-KIA Bastogne), S/Sgt. Spencer R. Hayes (KIA Holland), Joe Bass (KIA Korea), John R. O'Keefe, Rudy Korvas, Arthur Sherman, John Zeilmeier, and Glen Haley. Others could be, subject to confirmation, Alvie K. Griffith (KIA Holland), John Henry Poe, Leroy Prahm (KIA Normandy), Joseph Rippy (Co. HQ, KIA Bastogne). Their motto was Death before Dishonor.

One evening in Normandy, immediately after the invasion, Rudy Korvas entered a barn and surprised a sleeping German. The two men fought with bare hands and Rudy killed him. He took the soldier's *Soldbuch* (pay book) and tore out the photo. Until his death in 2002, Rudy kept the picture of this German on him. His relatives say that he often looked at it, without ever giving any explanation. Rudy was wounded during the assault on Hill 30 south of Carentan on June 13, 1944.

Above: Rudy Korvas in France at the end of the war, with Francis "Gus" Brown, an unidentified soldier and John Roberts (Mark Bando)

Below, left: Rudy Korvas, less famous than the Filthy 13 (no Mohawk haircut) the Dirty 13 were a very closely-knit bunch of friends in 1st platoon, F/501st.

Below: The Beaumont and Angoville-au-Plain sector would see for two full days some cruel examples of hedgerow fighting and hand-to-hand combat between German and American paratroopers.

Bottom: The 501st collar insignia. (Private collection)

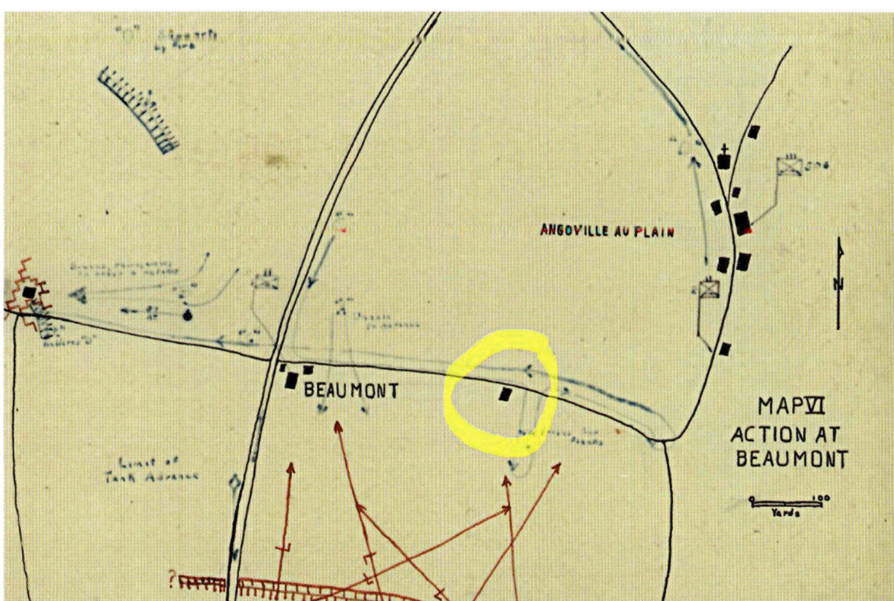

Taken prisoner in the early hours of the invasion, Johnny Gibson would witness first-hand as a medic the sufferings of his fellow POWs driven mercilessly to the rear to Saint Lô and Starvation Hill. Non-walking wounded would be sent to *Front Stalag 221* in Rennes where they would be liberated by the the US Army in August. Located in the Jean Maté children's school, this *stalag* saw quite a lot of US Airborne soldiers. Johnny Gibson reached the *stalag* at the end of July, having been retained as a medic by his German captors all the way to Mortain. The 35th Evacuation Hospital was moved from Carentan to Rennes on 4 August and, after an entire night moving in trucks, it was set up and became operational on the 5th, treating 600 liberated prisoners of war, most of whom were in a bad physical condition.

John W. Gibson; From Paratroops to Mister Arizona

John W. "Johnny" Gibson was born on August 27, 1921 in Humbolt, South Dakota. He died in Arizona in 2010. He joined the US Army on September 4, 1942 in Tucson, Arizona, and asked to join the paratroops. He trained at Toccoa before attending the Parachute School in Fort Benning with G/506th. A sportsman, he was interested in everything related to fitness and joined the regimental boxing team.

He jumped into Normandy on D-Day as a medic with the 101st Airborne, attached to HQ Company of the 3/506th. He was captured at daybreak on 6 June and taken to Rennes where he was liberated by Patton's armies on 4 August 1944. He was thus able to rejoin his unit and jump into Holland and he also took part in the encirclement at Bastogne. He was shot in the lung and liver on 9 January near Noville on the Belgian Ardennes, as he was attending to the wounds of Captain Jim Morton. He would spend eleven months in hospital before being demobilized on 5 December with the rank of sergeant.

He landed in a field on the edge of a farm, not far from Carentan, probably on the edge of Saint-Côme-du-Mont. As a medic, his was only armed with a knife. His Red Cross armband stood out in the night and he preferred to remove it for fear of being spotted by the many Germans who were shooting all around him. By activating his "cricket", he managed to be recognized by his friend Charles Lee who had jumped just before him, and George Rosie, of the 81 mm mortar platoon. George Rosie was a strong guy who could hold an 81 mm mortar barrel in each hand and at arm's length. The three men saw a C-47 in flames crash. Quickly joined by four men of their "stick" (a group of between 15 and 20 paratroopers embarked on the same plane), they made their way towards their objective, the bridges at Brévands. It was then that they come face to face with a large group of Germans – nearly a hundred men. Privates Abbey and Ronzani fell under the bursts of machine-guns. Gibson, and his friends Rosie and Swanson were captured. Only Lee momentarily managed to escape. He was quickly surrounded and shot. Abbey and Ronzani were dying, without Gibson being allowed to approach them and tend to them. He was taken under guard towards Carentan. Entering the town, he was brutally insulted and jostled by a woman who spat in his face. He spent the night in a pig shelter. The next day, he saw Charles K. Lewis, an Idaho Native American who had lost his right leg, in a cart. It was the beginning a long walk through Normandy to *Stalag 221* in Rennes for Johnny. It was there that he was liberated by American troops in early August, 1944.

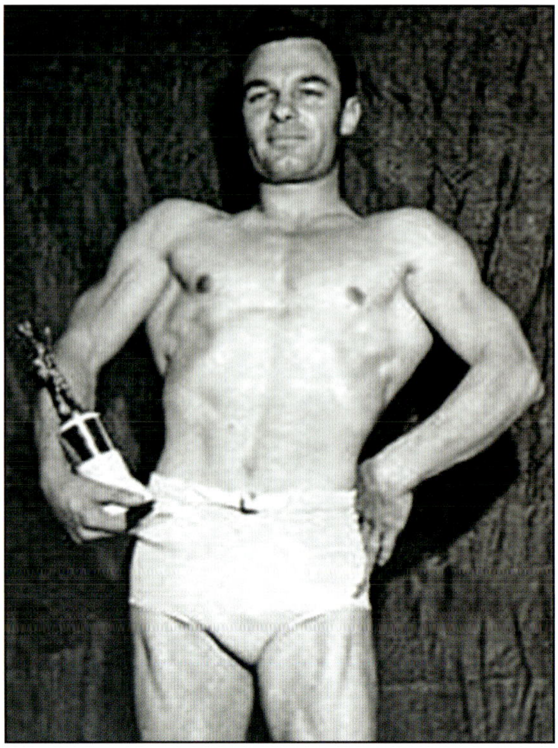

He resumed his role as Medic at HQ 3/506th, and jumped over Holland as part of Market. Then came Bastogne, and his terrible wound of January 9, 45.

Back in the United States, and after long hospital stays, he recovered and became, in 1950 and 1951, Mister Arizona.

They were the enemy... Fallschirmjäger-Regiment 6 and the Screaming Eagles

At the time of D-Day, the defense of Carentan was ensured by the 3,457 men of *Fallschirmjäger-Regiment 6*. Led by *Major* Friedrich August Freiherr von der Heydte, this parachute regiment had recently been formed at Koeln Wahn using a veteran cadre, but also with very young recruits. It was positioned around Carentan with, to the north, an *Ost-Truppen* battalion made up of Eastern volunteers, either Russians or other eastern people, but in this case, Georgians.

F.J.-Rgt. 6. comprised of three rifle battalions, each equipped with 18 machine-guns and three 80 mm mortars. Each battalion also had a heavy weapons company with 12 machine-guns, four 80 mm mortars and two howitzers. In support, the Regiment could also rely on three extra companies, the heavy mortar *13.Kp*. Armed with 12 cm mortars and its 8 machine-guns, the *14.-(Panzerjäger) Kompanie* (anti-tank), and its four 75 mm anti-tank guns, 34 *Panzerschrecks*, and six machine-guns. And the *15. Kp.* (*Pioniere*), an engineers company with its two 80 mm mortars and 6 machine-guns, but also flame-throwers. On the other hand, however, the Regiment was cruelly lacking in transportation.

On 6 June in the Carentan sector, *Generalleutnant* Marcks gave the Regiment a zone to cover from Lessay to Périers, including Raids, Saint-Georges de Bohon, Méautis and Baupte, making an area of 35km by 20 at the foot of the Cotentin peninsula. As early as 4 June, numerous signs alerted the Regiment to a possible invasion. Alsace-born soldiers who served as drivers deserted in droves. Telephone lines were cut and the the railroad line south of Périers sabotaged. At 22:30 on 5 June, aerial observation at Cherbourg notified the presence of a large naval and air activity. At 23:00, von der Heydte was alerted and told of these large concentrations of planes and ships in the Channel. Shortly after midnight, the 1st battalion of *F.J.-Rgt. 6* (commanded by *Hauptmann* Emil Preikschat), signaled the arrival of the first paratroopers in the Raids sector. They took their first 101st Airborne Division prisoners. The III battalion, in the Saint-Georges-de-Bohon sector, also reported the capture of American paratroopers. At around 6 in the morning on 6 June, general Marcks ordered von der Heydte to *"mop up the sector south of Carentan, and to attack the forces that had landed between Carentan and Sainte-Mère-Eglise"*. The III battalion was then still occupied in looking for paratroopers that had dropped south of the Carentan – Périers road. Von der Heydte carried out a reconnaissance on a motorbike as far as Saint-Côme-du-Mont. From the church tower, he could see the invasion fleet. He ordered his I and II battalions to join him from their assembly area at Méautis. *Hauptmann* Rolf Mager's II was to advance on both sides of the RN 13 highway towards Sainte-Mère-Eglise, and wipe-out any enemy encountered along the way. The I battalion had to undertake this advance by moving towards Sainte-Marie-du-Mont. The 13th company remained behind, whilst the III battalion, led by *Hauptmann* Horst Trebes, stayed in the Carentan sector. At midnight on 6 June, the I battalion was at Sainte-Marie-du-Mont, whereas the II battalion was 500 meters south of Sainte-Mère. They took a large number of prisoners along the way. However, the large American airborne forces in the sector, both of the 101st and 82nd, regrouped behind the II battalion which soon found itself cut-off. Von der Heydte spotted the danger and ordered his two battalions to halt their advance and regroup in a defensive arc around Saint-Côme-du-Mont. The II battalion sent notification that this order had been received and put it into application. However, the I battalion remained out of touch, both by radio and runner. American pressure towards Saint-Côme increased on 7 June and von der Heydte had to engage two companies from his third battalion to the east of Saint-Côme in order to protect the Carentan road against the arrival of American armor. From the morning of 8 June; the Americans, supported by strong artillery concentrations, infiltrated everywhere towards Saint-Côme and the German defenses fell apart. The *Fallschirmjäger* fell back towards Carentan, using the RN13 highway, but also the railroad line. Von der Heydte gave the order to blow the last bridge over the Douve and regrouped his forces to defend Carentan. Emil Preikschat's I battalion was wiped out on 7 June at Hell's Corner as it tried to reach Carentan via Brévands bridges. Only 25 men, led by lieutenant Stenzel, reached the town

Above: Alexander Uhlig, *16. Kompanie*, *F.J. Reg 6*. A veteran of Poland and Crete and a company commander in Carentan. Holder of the Knight's Cross of the Iron Cross medal, he became a POW during the Battle of Normandy. He could not wait to go home after the war and escaped from his POW camp in England. He died in 2008.

Below: the German parachutist badge was created in 1936 by Herman Göring. Parachutists would receive it after their sixth jump. (Private Collection)

Below: German paratroopers captured in the Carentan area. (US NARA)

Bottom: the *17. SS-Panzergrenadier-Division* commander, Werner Ostendorff, confers with von der Heydte south of Carentan on 12 June. They would immediately launch their counter-attack to regain the city. (DR)

4. "We're taking Carentan!"

Due to its location halfway between the two beaches of Omaha and Utah, on a major road and rail hub, the small town of Carentan, at the foot of the Cotentin peninsula, was identified at a very early stage by both allied and German high commands as crucial to the outcome of the invasion battle. The ferocity of the fighting, which led to the taking and securing of Carentan from 8 to 13 June, testifies to the city's highly strategic interest. On June 9 Lieutenant-General Omar Bradley, commander of the US 1st Army, asked the commander of the VII US Corps, Major General J. Lawton Collins, responsible for the capture of the Cotentin and Cherbourg, to deal with Carentan first in order to link up as soon as possible the two beachheads of Omaha and Utah. Ike Eisenhower himself insisted on this point as early as 7 June. Feld Marschall *Erwin Rommel also saw the danger. He ordered* Major *Baron von der Heydte's* Fallschirmjäger-Regiment 6. *to* "fight to the last man to hold Carentan!" 17. SS-Panzergrenadier-Division "Götz von Berlichingen" *undertook a route march from Thouars to Carentan with orders* "to throw the Americans into the sea". *On June 9, 1944, Max Taylor, Commanding Officer of the 101st Airborne announced to Collins that all the objectives of his unit had been achieved. Collins retorted curtly,* "Awright, now, let's take Carentan!"

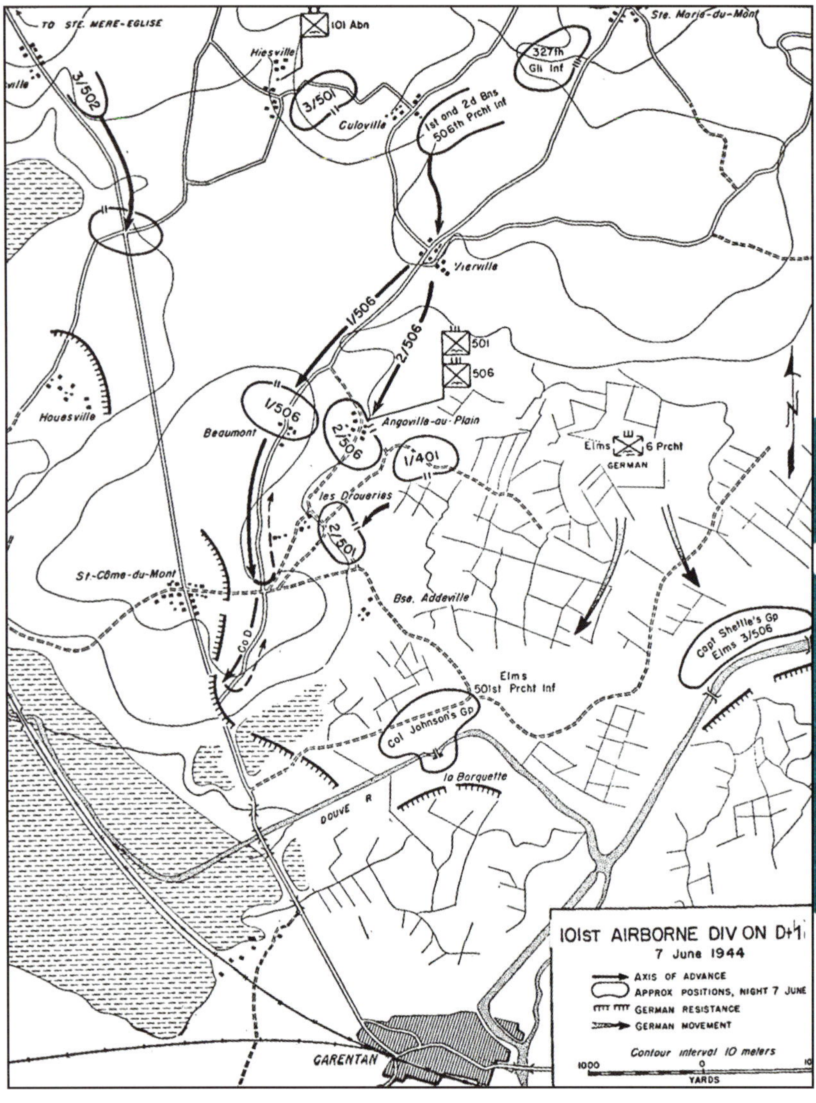

Mike Marquez was a member of the Filthy13, the Demolition men of the Regimental Headquarters of the 506th PIR. He also was a talented cartoonist, who would depict in humorous ways his brothers in arms for the regimental scrapbook. (Mike Marquez)

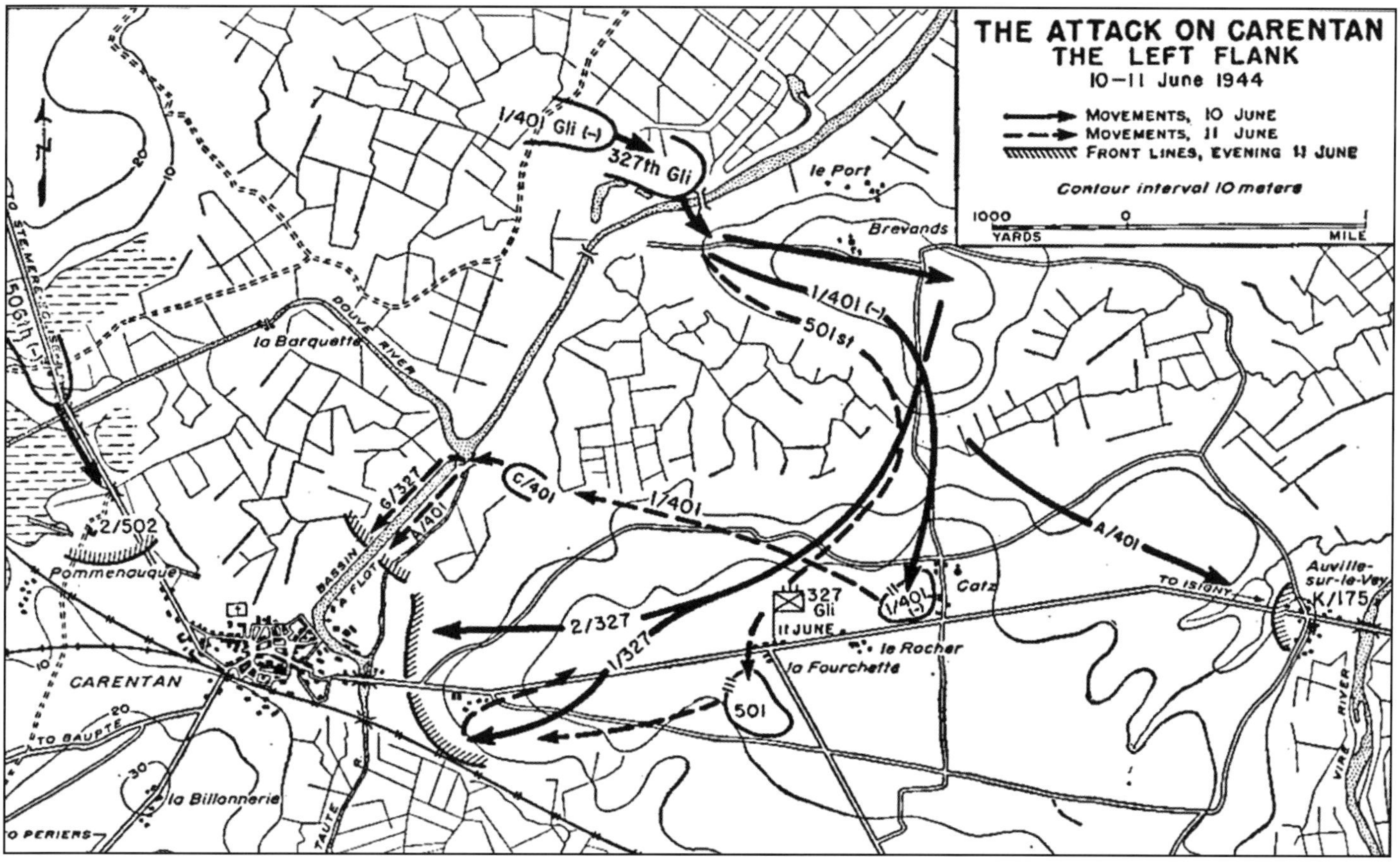

Forward...

On the evening of June 8, 1944, the 101st Airborne Division had completed all missions assigned to it on D-Day. Its 502nd Parachute Regiment guarded the right flank along the Douve river, its 506th Parachute Regiment deployed along the road between St-Côme-du-Mont and Sainte-Mère-Eglise, and his 327th Glider Regiment (GIR) occupied the left flank facing Brévands. His 501st Parachute Regiment was in divisional reserve and guarded the left flank to the east of the 327th GIR.

On the evening of June 9th, the 101st Airborne was instructed to take Carentan to connect the beachheads of the V and VII Corps that had landed at Omaha and Utah Beach.

Air patrols seemed to indicate that Carentan was only slightly defended and a plan to surround the city was decided, with the 502nd PIR on the right, and the 327th from Brévands on the left. The first phase of the attack was entrusted to the 3/502nd Parachute Infantry Regiment, ordered at 9 pm on June 9 to attack Carentan by the highway (former N13) coming from St Côme-du-Mont and which crossed the flooded areas. A three-sided encirclement was then planned, which involved ALL of the Division's regiments, the 327th GIR arriving by the tidal basin to the northeast, the 501st crossing the Vire-Taute canal at St Hilaire-Petitville to the east, taking Hill 30 and joining the 506th PIR south of the city. On the night of June 9 to 10, as the 3rd Battalion of the 502nd PIR continued its bloody assault at N° 4 bridge on Purple Heart Lane (former N13) at the entrance to Carentan, the 327th crossed the Douve aboard boats, inflatable tires or even by wading across. Quickly joined by the 401st, these glider borne troops would be the first Americans to set foot on the right bank of the Douve.

Saint-Côme-du-Mont fell into American hands on the evening of 8 June. The German paratroopers, and remnants of the *91. Luftlande-Division* retreated using the railroad bridge west of the town, and the N13 highway, destroying the Douve bridge. Protected on three sides by flooded marshlands, Carentan was a fortress that was skillfully reinforced by the Germans.

Fort Benning, March 1941, Omar Bradley, commander of the Infantry School, hands out the very first paratrooper badges. John Michaelis is already there, second from the right. (US Army)

John Hershey Michaelis, CO 502nd PIR; a pioneer of the US Airborne in Carentan...

John Hershey Michaelis was born on August 20, 1912 in San Francisco. He jumped to Normandy as Executive Officer (Deputy) of the 502nd PIR, commanded by Colonel George Van Horn Moseley. He was then Lieutenant Colonel and could be proud to be, at 32 years old, one of the pioneers of the US Airborne. He appeared among the very first cadres of the first parachute battalion of the US Army. In this photo dated March 1941, he was one of the first 300 recipients of Parachute wings, designed by William Pelham Yarborough. Omar Bradley can be seen on the left of the photo, at the time commander of the Infantry School of Fort Benning. On his left, is Major Bud Miley, commander of the 501st PIB, who later took command of the 17th Airborne.

Michaelis landed in Normandy near Saint-Germain-de-Varreville. He then went with his group from RHQ/502nd to Audouville-la-Hubert and Blosville. He took part in the attack west towards Houesville where fierce fighting against German paratroopers took place. Colonel Moseley broke his leg on landing. The fiery 502nd historic leader led the fighting from a wheelbarrow. General Anthony McAuliffe observed the scene at Saint-Côme-du-Mont and decided to relieve Moseley of his command and ordered him to return to England. Michaelis took charge of the Regiment. He later said "*Moseley was like a crazy man. On two occasions he threatened me with his Colt .45...*" Michaelis coordinated the dramatic actions of his 1st and 3rd battalions along Purple Heart Lane and up to the Cabbage Patch. He received the Silver Star in Carentan.

On September 22, 1944, he was in Holland at the head of the 502nd. A German shell exploded just above his command post at Schindel. 14 senior officers including Michaelis were wounded. Michaelis was evacuated but he returned for the Battle of the Bulge, as Chief of Staff of the 101st. He commanded the 27th Infantry Regiment in Korea and was Eisenhower's aide-de-camp from 1947 to 1948.

One of the first paratroopers and also one of the first to receive the first batch of Silver Wings designed in 1941 by Captain W.P. Yarborough, John Michaelis would rise through the ranks and naturally "inherit" the 502nd PIR after Georges van Horn Moseley broke his leg on D-Day. He is one of the dozen paratrooper executive officers of the very first paratroop battalion in the US Army who would go on to become generals by the end of their careers. (US Army)

A Carentan hero, Lieutenant Colonel Robert George Cole, 3/502nd Commanding Officer, posthumous Medal of Honor!

His name is inextricably linked to the town of Carentan and the battle to liberate the town in June 1944. Lieutenant Colonel Robert George Cole was the only soldier of the 101st Airborne to receive the Medal of Honor in the entire division in Normandy, as stipulated by its commander, Max Taylor, as a reward for a unique feat, a bayonet charge against the German command post located at the Ingouf farm on the edge of Carentan. Bob Cole never had the satisfaction of receiving his medal. He was killed near Best in Holland by a sniper bullet through his temple, on Monday, September 18, 1944, while trying to place orange reconnaissance panels on the ground to prevent his men from being strafed by American P47s. A trooper of I/502, Robert Boyce, saw the German sniper run from a distant farm and killed him. The 3/502, greatly affected by the loss of its leader, had the satisfaction of knowing Cole's death had been avenged. In a strange coincidence, the two 101st Airborne Medal of Honor recipients, Bob Cole and Joe Mann, both belonged to the 502nd PIR, and were both killed at Best! Lt. Col. Robert Cole landed near Sainte-Mère-Eglise. He gathered together 70 to 75 men, mainly of the 506th, including Lt. Dick Winters (E 506) and a dozen men, but also from the 505th and 508th PIR and headed to Saint-Martin-de-Varreville and to the battery that was the 502nd's objective. An hour later, he encountered a convoy of 5 (4 according to Koskimaki) carts laden with saddles for horses and mines. He seized it and killed a dozen Germans, but in the confrontation the S-4 of Major J W Vaughn's regiment was killed. The troopers grabbed the wagons and pushed on towards the empty and destroyed battery. Among the extremely small number of men to follow him in the bayonet charge against the German *Fallschirmjäger* command post on the morning of June 11, 1944, was his radio operator, another "Bob", Robert E. Doran, aged 21, from New Haven, Connecticut. Doran was killed by mortar fire a few minutes before Cole in Holland.

Bob Cole got to say a few words to Ike at Greenham Common before the big start. (US Army)

Left: Cole at Bragg. Note the absence of the Airborne tab above the Screaming Eagle patch, as the tab was only authorized by the end of August 1942. (US Army)

Cole was born on 19 March, 1915. He chose the army early on, following the example of his father, a colonel in the US Army. He graduated from West Point in 1939, (same class as Harry Kinnard and Julian Ewell!!) and was assigned to the 15th Infantry in 1940, where he served under the orders of a certain... Dwight David Eisenhower... He arrived at Fort Benning in March 1941 where he obtained his wings in the 501st Parachute Infantry Battalion. He was appointed Captain in March 42, Major in October 42, and Lt. Colonel in September 43. The American historian 101st Airborne Mark Bando drew a striking portrait of him: "*Lt. Col. Robert G. Cole, 3/502nd commander, was a tall, slender, muscular man with a strong, low-pitched voice that he never tried to mitigate. He wore his cap thrown back, and led his battalion with an iron fist. He managed to control his irreducible troopers by simple intimidation. One of his men, Ralph Kelly, was willing to admit that he was more afraid of Cole than the Germans.*"

At 6:15 am, Sunday, June 11, Cole requested a smoke screen. He informed the few men around him of his desire to take advantage of this smoke screen to charge Ingouf Farm with

Bob Cole was a 1939 West Point graduate, the same promotion as other great airborne commanders, Billy Boyle (517th), Harry Kinnard (501st), Edwin Ostberg (507th), Billy Turner (506th), Shields Warren (508th), Carl Buechner (506th). (US Army)

Survivors of the charge... the victors pose in front of the Ingouf farm, the former *Fallschirmjäger* command post. Lt. Col. Robert G. Cole, 1st. Sgt. Hubert Odom (DSC), G/502), Staff-Sgt. Robert P. O'Reilly (HQ, 3/502), and Maj. John P. Stopka (XO, 3/502). (US Army)

fixed bayonets. On his whistle, only about twenty men who had heard his order in the tumult and din of German fire, got up and followed him. John Stopka, his Executive Officer, relayed the order and rushed forward, followed by about 50 men from H and G Companies, and HQ 502nd PIR. Joel Mehall, Albert Kushmerick, Bernard Sterno and Robert Doran, Cole's radio operator, were among them. Three men of the 377th PFAB, which had been decimated after disastrous drops, managed to reach St Côme-du-Mont from Valognes. They were ordered to fight as simple infantrymen, and became involved in these events. These were Sergeant Arthur Parker, William Brown and Crowley. Sergeant Kenneth M. Specker and Private Roach were the first to reach Ingouf Farm. They blew the lock and rushed into the house, pursuing two Germans trying to escape via the back door. Lt. Edward A Provost followed Cole in the charge with 9 men. With 5 survivors he attacked a pillbox between Ingouf Farm and the Madeleine. With the T5 James O. Brune, they killed the defenders with their bayonets. 150 men from 3/502 arrived at the farm. They dug in along the hedgerows on either side of the farm. Cole sent a messenger for Lt. Colonel Patrick F. Cassidy to send his 1st Battalion, 502nd as reinforcements. Then began the battle of the Cabbage Patch to widen the defensive perimeter around Ingouf Farm which was now Robert Cole's command post.

A bayonet charge that would earn Bob Cole a Congressional Medal of Honor.

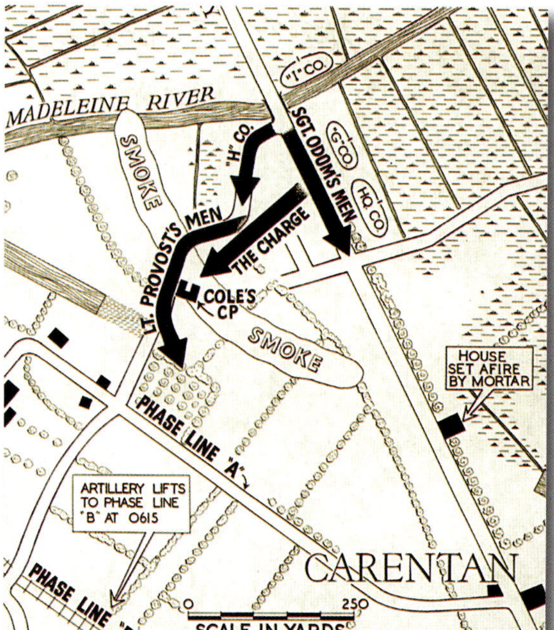

Vincent Utz, HQ 506th; a Hero before, during and after the war

Vincent "Vinnie" Utz was a hero for two reasons. A US University Football Star born in Connecticut, he was recruited by Rutgers University. He quickly became captain of the US football team in the early 1940s as a fullback. The star of the team, he was nicknamed "Wizard of Utz". He enlisted in 1941 and joined the 101st Airborne. Assigned to the 506th PIR, he joined the S-2 platoon of the Regiment which was tasked with gathering enemy intelligence. He was twice promoted corporal, but each time demoted after ending up in cells during furlough in London.

As a member of the S-2 section, he made the famous invasion "sand tables" , incredibly realistic models of the jump zones that every soldier had to memorize in the days preceding the invasion. He recalled having to trample on them to destroy them a few hours before embarking on the plane. He jumped from the same plane as Bob Sink, the boss of the 506th PIR who made him blacken his face using soot from the C-47's exhaust. He landed in an orchard on the edge of his Drop Zone, between Hiesville and Blosville. He remained hanging in a tree for a moment. He had jumped with his rifle already assembled and stuck under his arm. He managed to free himself and fell onto another S-2 platoon member, S/Sgt. Gunther Haiman, a Jew of Austrian origin. In the dark, he called out with the password "Flash" (to which Haiman should have answered with "Thunder"), but in his great confusion, Haiman answered "*Kamerad*" in his native language! Later, Vinnie briefly found his commanding officer, Captain Ed "Frosty" Peters, who was killed soon after. He stayed with Sink on a farm all day on June 6th.

Vinnie earned a Bronze Star in Normandy and a Silver Star in Holland during a reconnaissance patrol in which he escaped thanks only to a young Dutchman who gave him his bicycle. Two days after the beginning of the Battle of the Bulge at Bastogne, Vinnie lost an arm when a shell exploded. He was evacuated before the encirclement and was repatriated to the US aboard the Queen Mary.

He recovered from his wound and found work with Johnson and Johnson. In 1966, a fire broke out at his father's home in Metuchen, New Jersey. He was suffering from Parkinson's disease and Vinnie, although deprived of an arm, rushed to his rescue. He saved his life but succumbed to the fire.

Vinnie Utz, Bronze Star Medal in Normandy, Silver Star in Holland. Vinnie could have played with the 101st Airborne football team, whose coach in England happened to be... Robert Cole.

Top: Aerial view of the northern sector of Carentan, looking towards Saint-Côme-du-Mont and the four rivers to be crossed before reaching the cabbage patch and the Ingouf farm. From north to south: the Jourdan, the Douve, the Groult and the Madeleine rivers.

Center: A 1944 view of the Ingouf farm, in the foreground, and the four bridges in the middle of the marshes.

Bottom: The bridge over the Jourdan, blocked by obstacles such as this Belgian Pointet gate.

Purple Heart Lane

Bridge No. 2, beyond the place known as Ponts d'Ouve, and which spanned the Douve, was destroyed by the Germans on the evening of 8 June. The mission to install a temporary crossing was entrusted to the Engineers of the 326th AEB on the evening of 9 June. Shortly after midnight on June 10th, Lt. Ralph B. Gehauf (intelligence officer of the 3/502) and 9 soldiers carried out a reconnaissance mission along the RN 13. They crossed the 4 bridges from Les Ponts d'Ouve to Carentan. They did not trigger any enemy reaction. Gehauf was accompanied by Sgt. O'Reilly, Cpl. Martin Washko, Tony Diaz of Leon (WIA), Carl Dayak and James White, acting as scouts.

At 4 o'clock on Saturday, June 10, the 3/502 was in front of bridge N ° 2. It had still not been repaired and the Engineers refused to intervene under the fire of the 88. Cole was furious. The assault was postponed and the battalion returned to Les Quesnils. Gehauf, still beyond bridge No. 4 and seeing nothing coming, also returned to Les Quesnils at 5:30 in the morning, not without having triggered a strong enemy response.

It was not until around 2 pm on Saturday, June 10, that Cole himself, with the help of a few soldiers, established a rope and plank bridge on bridge No.2, in the absence of the Engineers of the 326h AEB. At 1 pm that Saturday, June 10, the 3/502nd PIR resumed its advance.

At 3 pm, the G Company led by Lt. Clements crossed this temporary bridge No.2 in single file and began the perilous along the road which was covered by German fire. An hour later, Clements and his men were at bridge No.4.

At 18:00 hours, the whole battalion of about 700 men was stretched out from Ponts d'Ouve to bridge No. 4 over La Madeleine. The men were subjected to the incessant firing of machine-guns that were spread out on both sides of the road, as well as artillery and mortar fire. The troopers were totally exposed and could down even dig in along the roadway.

At 23:30 on this Saturday, June 10, the entire 3/502 cluttered the road near bridge No. 4 over La Madeleine. It was at that point that one or two *Luftwaffe* planes appeared and dropped bombs on Item Company which was caught out in the open on the road. The planes then made another sweep with their machine-guns. 1/502 suffered 30 casualties.

The 3rd Battalion continued its effort, crossing the Groult (bridge No.3) and reaching bridge No. 4 over the La Madeleine river. The Germans blocked the road here by placing a “Belgian gate” across the small bridge. The troopers could pass only one by one under the fire of the machine-guns whose bullets ricocheted against the bars of the gate creating sparks in the night. G and H Companies, and part of HQ/3rd, followed I Company through this mousehole and the soldiers rushed to find refuge in the ditches north of the Cabbage Patch, on either side of the Carentan road.

Beyond the last bridge, No. 4, was a large open field. A farm at one end served as a command post for German paratroopers. The Germans had dug trenches and bunkers in the hedgerows on the south side of the field where they could position a large number of men. At 3:30 am on Sunday, June 11, Captain Cecil Simmons and his 84 officers and men of H Company, undertook to cross No. 4 bridge and deploy along the road to Pommenauque in hedges and ditches. G Company followed with only 60 men.

The HQ/3rd Battalion had 121 troopers. Item Company was reduced in less than 24 hours from 80 soldiers and 5 officers to 21 men and 2 officers. Lieutenant Colonel Cole gave the order to withdraw.

Big “Cec”, Cecil L. Simmons, H/502nd; a survivor of Purple Heart Lane, he succeeded Cole and Stopka as head of 3/502nd PIR

Cecil Simmons commanded H Company of the 3rd Battalion, 502nd PIR in Normandy. A policeman in civilian life, he had also served in the Military Police before joining the airborne forces. He had made himself very unpopular with his men since his inaugural speech, warning the tough guys that as a former MP, he knew how to treat the strong-headed soldiers. But “Big Cec” quickly became one of the most respected cadres of the battalion. As early as June 8, he distinguished himself in Normandy during a German counterattack led by *Infanterie-Regiment 243.* in the Houesville sector. His tenacity that day, in the face of forces that were superior in number earned him a Bronze Star. Simmons’ action during the bayonet charge led by his battalion commander, Robert G. Cole, at the German command post entrenched in Ingouf Farm, did not go unnoticed either.

Beyond the last bridge, N°4, on the RN 13 highway, overlooking the Madeleine, was a large open field. A farm at the far-end was being used as a command post by German parachutists. The hedgerows along the southern side of the field had been fortified by the Germans with trenches and bunkers that could hold a large number of men. At 3.30 am on Sunday, 11 June, Captain Cecil Simmons and 84 officers and men from H Company, began crossing bridge N°4 and deployed along the Pommenauque road in the hedgerows and ditches. G Company followed with only 60 men.

HQ/3rd Battalion had 121 troopers. We should be reminded that Item Company was understrength, reduced in the space of 24 hours from 80 men and 5 officers to 21 men and 2 officers, following the terrible day of 10 June. Lieutenant-Colonel Cole ordered it to withdraw.

At 6:15 am, Sunday, June 11, Cole requested a smoke screen. He informed the few men around him of his desire to take advantage of this smoke screen to charge Ingouf Farm with fixed bayonets. On his whistle, only about twenty men who had heard his order in the tumult and din of German fire, got up and followed him. John Stopka, his Executive Officer, relayed the order and rushed forward, followed by about 50 men from H and G Companies, and HQ 502nd PIR. Joel Mehall, Albert Kushmerick, Bernard Sterno and Robert Doran, Cole's radio operator, were among them, as well as “Big Cec”. The first men to reach the farm were Sergeant Kenneth M. Sprecker and Private Roach were the first to reach Ingouf Farm. They blew the lock and rushed into the house, pursuing two Germans trying to escape via the back door.

Lt. Edward A Provost followed Cole in the charge with 9 men. With 5 survivors he attacked a wooden pillbox between Ingouf Farm and the Madeleine. With T5 James O. Brune, they killed the defenders with their bayonets.

In all, 150 men of H, G Companies and HQ Company of the 3/502 reached the farm and dug in along the hedgerows around it.

Cecil Simmons survived all of the Regiment’s the battles. He succeeded John Stopka (killed in the Ardennes) as commander of 3/502nd, with the

Bottom: Cecil Simmons, “Big Cec”, a hero of the fighting at Purple Heart Lane and the Cabbage Patch.

Above: Simmons talks with his commanding officer, Robert Cole, in a street of Carentan, a few days after the battle.

Right: Fairbairn-Sykes knife, similar to the one Simmons mentioned…

rank of major. He would go on to become a general in the Michigan National Guard.

As night fell on the evening of 8 June in Houesville, Simmons heard the sound of a struggle in a grove on the edge of his company’s bivouac. He stepped forward, unsheathing his two fighting knives, an M3 attached to his ankle, and a British commandos Fairbairn pattern fighting knife, attached to his forearm. He found one of his junior officers struggling with a German. As he prepared to intervene, he spotted a movement behind his back. Another German threw himself on him. Simmons was quicker and pushed his M3 into the man’s abdomen. At the same time, he stabbed the German in the face with all his strength with his Fairbairn to the point that the blade stuck in his eye socket and could not be pulled out. He casually wiped the blade of his M3 on his sleeve and put it back in the sheath. The next day, he opened a can and began to eat with the tip of the same M3. The officer he had rescued the day before noticed it and grimaced with disgust. “Big Cec” shrugged and said, *“So what! I wiped it on my sleeve...”*

Lt. Colonel Ben Weisberg's helmet. The 377th PFAB was attached to the 502nd PIR for most of the war. (Mark Bando)

Bottom right: Melvin Spruiell, an artillery observer in the heart of the fighting (Mark Bando)

Below: Lt. Colonel Benjamin Weisberg, commanding officer of the 377th Parachute Field Artillery Battalion, would lose his job at the end of August 1944, officially for passing over secret documents to his father, documents he wanted to save as souvenirs. Unofficially, it seems that he punched Max Taylor out of anger for losing so many men due to bad drops on 6 June.

An artillery observer, Melvin Morton Spruiell

Lieutenant Melvin Morton Spruiell is one of the heroes of Carentan. He jumped over Normandy as F.O., Artillery Forward Observer of the 377th Parachute Field Artillery Battalion. This battalion, commanded by Lt. Col. Ben Weisberg, suffered certainly the worst drop of all Airborne D-Day units. Some of its members fell in the immediate vicinity of Cherbourg. Its losses were considerable, not to mention its 12 75 mm Howitzers... of which only one would be found and used. Melvin M. Spruiell and his counterpart, Captain St Julien Rosemond managed to find and use two Russian guns taken from the Germans. With their only remaining Howitzer, despite everything, they were still able to support the attacks on St.-Côme-du-Mont. Next, they naturally become platoon leaders of a group of paratroopers for the assault on Carentan. In the image of Robert Cole who charged on the Ingouf Farm, Spruiell rushed into furious assaults against German machine-gun nests that protected Carentan in the Cabbage Patch area. It was during one of these assaults that he was mortally wounded. His battalion CO, Ben Weisberg, immediately decided to nominate him posthumously for a Distinguished Service Cross. Alas! Weisberg, back in England, fell out of favor and was returned stateside. The recommendation was forgotten and lost.

It was the historian of the 101st, Mark Bando, who later found it in Weisberg's papers. He passed it on to Spruiell's brother who successfully solicited his congressman to follow it up!

Melvin Morton Spruiell was posthumously awarded the DSC more than 50 years after the events and his tragic death.

Taking the Marmion farm was a short, yet violent affair, involving a mixed bag of soldiers from different units in the 101st, and led by Major John Stopka. (US Army)

Lt. Colonel Patrick "Hopalong" Cassidy, from Marmion Farm to Ingouf Farm

Patrick Cassidy made a strong impression during the first three days of his 1/502nd's engagement to the northern sector of the 101st Airborne zone at Foucarville and Ravenoville. His skill and efficiency made his battalion one of D-Day's most successful. S.L.A. Marshall even claimed that Cassidy did "*the best job for America on D-Day!*" However, he had not finished with Normandy since his battalion was, as of the evening of June 9, appointed to support the assault of Robert Cole's 3/ 502nd along Purple Heart Lane to Carentan. The jump and 9 days of fighting since D-Day had nevertheless cut strongly into its ranks, even before the attack on Carentan. Most of the platoons had less than 30 men, some as few as 20. Most had only one officer and half of their NCOs. Nevertheless, Cassidy, in his turn, had to make his men cross one by one the Cointet gateway where Purple Heart lane ended at the La Madeleine bridge. The losses were terrible and the men who managed to cross took cover in any uneven ground that could offer shelter against the German fire. Sergeant Layton Black of C/502nd said: "*We had to cover almost 400 meters before finding any protection. We were completely uncovered, real sitting ducks for the enemy from the moment we started running. All along the roadway, and crossing the bridge, through the "Belgian gate". Crossing the bridge and leave the national highway to the farm (Ingouf editor's note). Leaving this road and crossing the field. Jumping over the waterlogged ditch. Running to the corner of the Cabbage Patch until you reach the hedge parallel to the national road. 400 meters of pure steel!* "

Company commanders Wallace Swanson and Fred Hancock, performed miracles, exhorting their men to fight the German parachutists who had made each hedge of the Cabbage Patch into small, well-sheltered fortresses, sometimes in hand-to-hand combat. It took the intervention of the American heavy artillery on the afternoon of June 11 to put an end to this grueling man-to-man confrontation, with the *Fallschirmjäger* pulling back one by one either towards Carentan or Pommenauque. Cassidy became Executive Officer of the 502nd in August 44, passing command of the 1/502nd to Lt. Colonel Thomas Sutliffe.

Layton Black: "The Last First Sergeant"

Left: Patrick Cassidy. His First Battalion, 502nd PIR supported 3/502nd in hand-to-hand fighting, in the patchwork of fields known as the cabbage patch along the RN 13 highway.

5. Fixed bayonets!

At 0430 hrs on Sunday 11th June 1944, it was HQ Company's turn to pass through the fencing blocking bridge N° 4 to spread out there facing the Ingouf Farm, which was the command post for the German parachutists from FJ. Reg. 6. Cole asked for artillery support from the observer, Captain Rosemead, who was in contact with the 377th Field Artillery Battalion, the 90th Battalion and the 65th Armored Field Artillery. Shells rained down around Ingouf Farm, but German gunfire continued.

At 0615 hrs, Cole requested a smoke barrage. He informed the few men around him that he wanted to take advantage of this smoke screen to lead a bayonet charge on Ingouf Farm. When he blew his whistle, only around twenty men stood up and followed him as they were the only ones to hear the order in the chaos and noise from the German guns. John Stopka, his Executive Officer, passed on the order and went in followed by fifty or so men from H, G and HQ companies. Joel Mehall, Albert Kushmerick, Bernard Sterno and Robert Doran, Cole's radio operator were among them.

The slow and deadly advance of Robert Cole's 3/502, along the barren, exposed causeway, swept by German machine-gun fire.

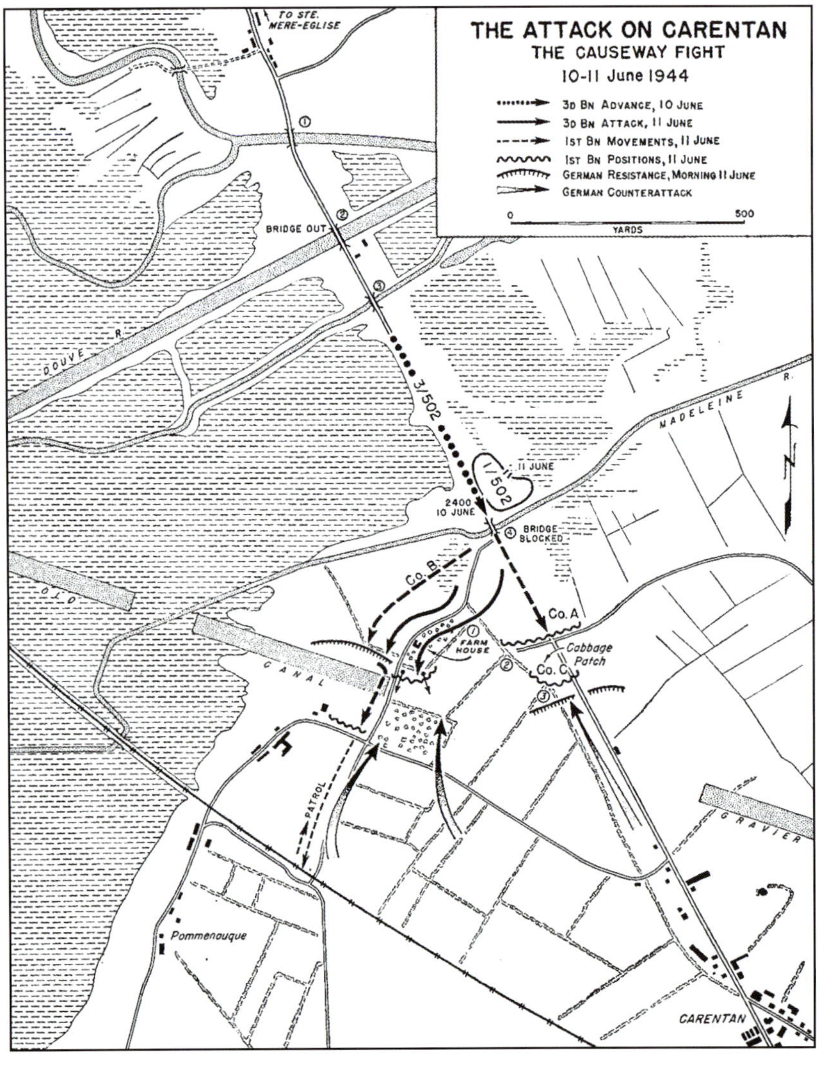

Three men from the 377th PFAB, which had been decimated in the disastrous parachute drops, managed to reach St-Côme-du-Mont from Valognes. They received the order to fight as simple infantrymen and got caught up in the events. They were the Sergeants, Arthur Parker, William Brown and Crowley.

Sergeant Kenneth M Sprecker and Private Roach (H Company) were the first to reach Ingouf Farm. They blew the lock apart and rushed into the house before chasing two Germans, who were trying to escape through the back door.

Lt Edward A Provost followed Cole's charge with 9 men. With five survivors, he attacked a pillbox between Ingouf Farm and la Madeleine. With the T5 James O. Brune, they killed the defenders using their bayonets.

150 men from 3/502 made it to the farm from H, G and HQ companies. They went to ground along the hedges on either side of the farm.

Cole sent a messenger to ask Lt Colonel Patrick F Cassidy to send his 1st battalion from the 502nd to support them. The cabbage patch battle then began with the aim of widening the defense perimeter around Ingouf Farm, which was now Robert Cole's command post.

The heavy losses suffered by the 3/502nd led the road between Carentan and St Côme to be given the nickname, Purple Heart Lane, a reference to the medal awarded to injured US Army soldiers. By the evening of 12th June, only 121 able-bodied men remained in Cole's battalion.

Bernard Sterno, H/502nd; a survivor from Purple Heart Lane in Carentan, deserter, and Red Army soldier…

What Private Bernard Sterno from H Company 502 PIR experienced gives a very good idea of what the men who followed Lt Col Robert Cole went through during the bayonet charge on Sunday 11th June, the US Army's first in Europe. Although his M1 had jammed, Sterno was one of the few to have followed Cole's run across open ground towards Ingouf farm. His Garand M-1 rifle had jammed and Bernard did not have a bayonet. Halfway there, Sterno noticed the body of a German soldier lying across a trench behind a bush. He could see a pistol was attached to the German's wrist. Sterno wanted the pistol, but afraid that the body might be booby trapped, he cut the cord with his knife. He then felt something hit a finger on his right hand. As he was wearing gloves, he did not immediately realize that he had been hit by a bullet which cut off one of his fingers. He recovered the pistol and continued to crawl forward. A little further on, he came across another man from H Company. He got close to him, but could see that the man had been shot in the chest and was dying. A medic joined him and pointed out to Sterno that blood was pouring out of his right hand. He bandaged it up and Sterno continued on his way. He then heard someone shouting out, "*Help me!*" It was his company's sergeant. Sterno crawled towards him. The sergeant had been shot in the stomach and legs. Close to him lay the medic who had just taken care of Sterno. He had dropped dead with a bullet in his head. Sterno grabbed his medical equipment and did his best to look after the sergeant. At that moment, the enemy fire doubled in intensity around the farm. Colonel Cole made signs to his men to get around the obstacle. Sterno managed to advance to around twenty meters behind the farm and joined other troopers all lined up in a ditch full of water. He then opened fire with an M1 taken from an wounded soldier. The bandage around his hand started to come off. Another medic appeared and looked at the injury, ordering him to go to the rear. There were many wounded men lying in the ditch alongside the road and Sterno said to himself that he had to help them. They begged him to stay with them and to call for a jeep to pick them up. But by then, the ditch and the road were under heavy 88 fire from Carentan. One man lying near Sterno lost an eye to shrapnel. He did not know if his eye was still in place and expressed his worries to Sterno. Sterno did not want to tell him the truth and replied: "*Well, even if you have lost it, you should be pleased you still have the other one...*" He prepared some cotton wool soaked in sulfonamide, and placed it on the wound. Then he looked after another injured man. Another 88 shell went whistling by. Sterno jumped into the ditch, but was too late. He felt "*something really heavy*" on his back, which felt like he had been kicked by a mule. He was not sure if he had been wounded again or whether it was just the blast from the explosion. In fact, an big shell splinter had entered his back and exited through the armpit. He would only find that out in the hospital ship the next day. The man who had lost his eye was screaming: "*My arm! My arm! My arm!*" Sterno was feeling groggy. When he looked at the man, he could see that his arm had been blown to smithereens in the explosion. Another man nearby who had still been alive a second before had lost half of his skull. Sterno had the impression that blood

502nd collar insignia. (Private collection)

was pouring down his back, but he was not sure. He told himself that it was probably the shock and his imagination. He glanced towards the injured men in the ditch. One man a few yards from him was bleeding from the ears, nose and mouth. He was still alive, but so shocked that he could only mutter a few incomprehensible words. Sterno told himself that he could not do much for any of these men. He crawled forward again towards bridge N°4 (la Madeleine – author's note). He saw a foxhole and slipped into it. Thirty seconds later a mortar shell fell close to the hole and his neck was hit by shrapnel, while an officer who was there was killed...

Captain Cecil Simmons's H/502 Company had gone on the attack on 11th June with 84 men. Only thirty were left by the evening.

On 17th September 1944, Bernard Sterno was still in hospital in England with a serious back wound from the large piece of shrapnel that went through his body close to his spine. He received the information that an important airborne operation involving his 101st Airborne had just taken place. He discreetly left the hospital and went to the camp where only the Service Corps remained. He made his way to one of the aerodromes and hung around the C 47s. Each day, supply missions were carried out. He bluffed his way into a crew, telling them that he was an expert in dropping equipment bundles. The crew were missing a member and agreed to take him aboard. On 21st September, he therefore found himself on his way to Holland to a supply zone for the 82nd Airborne close to Nijmegen. Sterno, doing exactly what he had promised, worked hard on board the plane. When the green light came on, he pushed the bundles out and to the amazement of the crew, also jumped with his white Air Corps parachute. From the ground, Germans and Dutchmen were watching the drop. The white parachute attracted their attention and the civilians and German soldiers rushed to the spot. Sterno landed in a little hollow, where for a moment he could not be seen by the German patrols. An elderly Dutchman arrived on his bicycle and told him to hop onto the luggage rack. Pedaling as fast as he could, the old man took Sterno to the American lines. From there he joined his H Company just as they were moving off once again down Hell's Highway, blocked between Veghel and St Oedenrode. The action of the squad leader was such that he was immediately promoted to sergeant. It was during this operation that Sterno was captured. He would spend the rest of the war in a *stalag*. After several escape attempts, he would finally be liberated by the Red Army.

In England, the hospital declared Sterno 'Awol' (Absent without Leave), and the Air Corps charged him with the theft of a parachute.

Bernard Sterno went through hell in Normandy. His father, a Polish immigrant, changed his name to Sterno after picking up Sterno brand can of soup in the cargo ship transporting him to the United States. (Mark Bando)

502nd Parachute Infantry Battalion

(since 1.07.1941 to 2.03.1942)

• CO: Major George P. Howell, Jr (1.07.1941 to 2.03.1942)

502nd Parachute Infantry Regiment (since 2.03.1942), widow makers

• CO: Lt. Col. George P. Howell, Jr (31.03.1942), Colonel George Van Horn "Old Moe" Moseley (since 04.1942, WIA 6.06.1944), Lt Col. John H. "Iron Mike" Michaelis (7.06.1944, WIA 22.09.1944), Lt Col. Steve A. "Silent Steve" Chappuis (22.09.1944)

• XO: Lt Col. John H. "Iron Mike" Michaelis (7.06.1944), Lt. Col. Allen W. Ginder (WIA 25.10.1944), Lt Col. Patrick F. "Hopalong" Cassidy (25.10.1944)

• Regimental S-4: Major J. W. Vaughan (KIA 6.06.1944)

• Regimental S-3: Lt. Col. Allen W. Ginder (7.06.1944)

• Assistant S-3: Captain Henry G. Plitt

• Regimental S-2: Captain George A. Buker

• Assistant S-2: 1st Lt. Robert G. Pick

• Regimental S-1: Captain Hugh Roberts

• Adjutant and Liaison Officer: Captain Evans C. Thornton

• Munitions Officer: Captain Carl E. Trimble

• Communications Officer: Captain Ivan G. Phillips

• Regimental Chaplain: Captain Raymond S. Hall

• Regimental Chaplain: Captain Joseph A. Andrejewski

• POW Interrogator: Lt. Col. Allen W. Ginder

• Regimental HQ Co: Captain Rudolph M. Jones

• Regimental Service Co: Captain Eldia R. Haire

1st Battalion, 502nd Parachute Infantry Regiment (1/502)

• CO: Lt Col. Patrick F. "Hopalong" Cassidy (25.10.1944), Captain Frank D. Hanlon (25.10.1944)

• XO: Major Thomas H. Sutliffe (22.09.1944)

• Adjutant: 1st Lt. Sidney R. Clary

• S-4: 1st Lt. Joseph F. Snecinski

• S-3: Captain James J. Hatch (1.01.1945)

• S-2: 2nd Lt. E. E. Gideon

• HQ Co: Captain James J. Hatch (1.01.1945)

• A Co: Captain Richard L. Davidson (KIA 6.06.1944), 1st/Lt. Wallace A. Swanson

• B Co: Captain Cleveland R. Fitzgerald (WIA 6.06.1944)

• C Co: Captain Fred A. Hancock, Captain George R. Cody, Captain John Dahlin

2nd Battalion, 502nd Parachute Infantry Regiment (2/502)

• CO: Lt Col. Steve A. "Silent Steve" Chappuis (22.09.1944), Lt. Col. Thomas Sutliffe (22.09.1944, WIA 1.01.1945, DOW), Major James J. Hatch (1.01.1945)

• XO: Captain Carlton P. Chandler

• Adjutant: 1st Lt. Hugh O. Roberts

• S-4: 1st Lt. John G. Callinan

• S-3: Captain Frank D. Hanlon (25.10.1944)

• S-2: 1st Lt. Glen E. Johnson

• HQ Co: Captain James R. Martin, Jr

• D Co: Captain Carl E. Trimble, Captain William A. Bolton (WIA)

• E Co: Captain Robert S. Dickson (do około 2 tygodnie przed 6.06.1944), Captain Fred O. Drennan (KIA 18.09.1944)

• F Co: Captain LeGrand K. Johnson, 1st Lt. Earl Hendricks (WIA 3.01.1945), Captain Raymond T. Smith

3rd Battalion, 502nd Parachute Infantry Regiment (3/502)

• CO: Lt Col. Robert G. Cole (KIA 18.09.1944), Major John Stopka (18.09.1944, KIA 14.01.1945), Captain Cecil L. Simmons (14.01.1945)

• XO: Major John P. Stopka (18.09.1944)

• Adjutant: 1st Lt. Ralph A. Watson Jr.

• S-4: 1st Lt. James V. Cauley

• S-3: Captain Edward J. Barrett

• S-2: 1st Lt. Ralph B. Gehauf

• HQ Co: Captain Raymond T. Smith (WIA 11.06.1944), Captain Frank Lillyman

• G Co: Captain Robert L. Clements (WIA 11.06.1944), Captain Ralph A. Watson Jr.

• H Co: Captain Cecil L. Simmons (14.01.1945), Captain Robert E. Jones

• I Co: Captain Frank Lillyman, Captain Ivan R. Hershner Jr, Captain Champ L. Baker

Major John P. Stopka, 3/502nd XO; the Mad Major of Carentan

John Stopka, originally from a Polish family from Sheridan, Wyoming, was given the nickname of the Mad Major in Normandy, probably because of his fearlessness when fighting. He was then Executive Officer of the third battalion of the 502nd PIR, under the command of Robert G. Cole. It was him that brought together the paratroopers from the 502nd near Ravenoville along with the 506th spread out in the marshland behind Utah Beach. He organized his own small group of around twenty men and attacked Marmion farm, a German stronghold on the southern edge of Ravenoville. The farm housed an MG 42 machine-gun, which fired on the paratroopers wandering around the marshes at daybreak on 6th June. After an hour and a half of fighting, the German defenders, totaling around thirty men, surrendered to the Americans. Stopka organized the defense of the farm and waited for the arrival of the troops from the 4th ID, who had just come ashore on Utah Beach.

On 11th June, he was alongside his CO, Bob Cole, when the latter ordered a bayonet charge on the German command post barricaded up at Ingouf farm on the northern edge of Carentan. Stopka is one of the few to have heard the order to attack and was one of the first to go on the attack. A bullet hit his helmet but was did not penetrate. The example he gave led to him being awarded a DSC, after he exposed himself to enemy fire throughout the morning, while telling his men to move out of their precarious shelter along La Madeleine and the RN 13 road.

Just like Cole, he personified the leadership of the American paratrooper officers who led from the front. Just like his boss, Stopka would not see the end of the conflict. Cole was killed in Holland on 18th September and Stopka was naturally given command of the 3/502nd. But on 14th January 1945, near Bourcy in the Belgian Ardennes, an American P-47 accidentally dropped a 500 pound bomb on American positions. Stopka was killed. Cecil Simmons, CO of Item Company, who was also involved in the fighting around Ingouf farm, would end up as CO of 3/502nd.

To justify his nickname of the Mad Major, we can mention an incident recounted by several witnesses. When Stopka, standing facing enemy fire, told his men to get out of the ditches to go on the attack, the CO of the Headquarters Company of the 3/506th, "Whispering" Smith, refused to move. Without batting an eyelid, Stopka fired on him, grazing his behind.

John P. Stopka received a Distinguished Service Cross for his actions on 11 June at bridge N°4. The citation reads: "*When the assault signal was given, he was the first man out, charging unprotected across the road towards enemy positions…*"

Captain Fred Alonzo Hancock, CO C/ 502nd PIR, 101st Airborne

Fred Hancock, born in 1910 in Oktaha, Oklahoma, was, in 1944, the eldest officer in the 502nd Parachute Infantry, apart from his commander in chief, George Van Horn Moseley. That is why he was never promoted beyond the rank of Major. He began his career in the airborne troops with the 81 mm Mortar Platoon, HQ company, 1st Battalion, 502nd Parachute Infantry, with whom he crossed the Atlantic to head for England. He was given command of Charlie Company in the 502nd just before D-Day. He jumped over Normandy on 6th June and landed near Le Haut Fornel, to the east of Beuzeville, where he immediately came under German fire. On Sunday 11th June, Bloody Sunday, following on from Robert Cole's bayonet charge, his battalion, led by Pat Cassidy, was involved in action along the RN 13 road, in an area of small fields, known as the "Cabbage Patch". He was wounded by grenade fragments thrown at close range by the German *Fallschirmjäger*. Fred Hancock had joined the National Guard, in the 45th Division, right at the start of the thirties. In 1934, he was given his commission as 1st Lieutenant, 10 years before being promoted to the rank of captain. He volunteered for the parachutists. His action at the Cabbage Patch led to him being awarded a Bronze Star, and a Purple Heart. His citation for the Bronze Star mentioned his achievements: "*On 11th June 1944 during the Battle of Carentan, Captain Hancock led his company to fight against a huge enemy force on open ground to take up position 60 yards from enemy lines. Captain Hancock skillfully placed his platoons in position to push back against the German counter-attacks. During this, he continually exposed himself to intense enemy fire and with no thought about his own safety, refused to retreat. Injured by an enemy grenade, he refused any medical assistance and continued to encourage his men to hold their line of defense, inflicting huge losses on the enemy...*"

Hancock would receive a Silver Star in Holland in September 1944 for similar actions in Sint Oedenrode. He would be seriously wounded there with a 9 mm bullet in the chest. He recovered from his wound and became S-2 in the 502nd (Intelligence Officer). The remembrance plaque at the Cabbage Patch Monument in Carentan mentions his name.

Bottom: Fred Hancock; his name is closely associated with the Cabbage Patch memorial in Carentan. He was the oldest officer in the Battalion. He commanded the 80 mm mortar squad in 1943. He was appointed Charley Company CO in England.

Right: summer style garrison cap belonging to Fred Hancock. (Mark Bando.)

Bottom, left: The 502nd PIR was the organic parachute regiment of the 101st from the moment of its activation in 1942.

6. And the Glidermen!

The 327th came ashore on Utah Beach, in the "Uncle Red" sector. Only the anti-tank platoon of HQ/327th arrived by glider in Mission Chicago at four in the morning on 6th June.

The lack of gliders forced the 327th, and their battalion in the 401st, to arrive in Normandy by sea. By the third week of May 1944, the men were confined to an assembly area in Wales, where they kept busy ensuring their equipment, weapons and radios were watertight. Only the anti-tank platoon would take part in the airborne assault. Six gliders would bring them in from Aldermaston.

The men of the 327th and the 401st left England on the afternoon of 5th June aboard LCIs. Following on from the 4th ID, they were to go ashore at Utah Beach on 6th June. The 401st was the first ashore at 18:00 hrs. The Headquarters Company of the 327th, with their CO George Wear, followed, but most of the 327th was unable to go ashore before 22:30 hrs. G Company would have to wait until around 15:00 hrs on the following day (7th June) due to difficult sea conditions. It was only on 7th June that the 327th and the remainder of the 401st were finally able to assemble ashore and march towards Sainte-Marie-du-Mont. The 401st was briefly attached to Bob Sink's 506th PIR to support his attack on St-Côme-du-Mont. Their chaplain, Father Steel, was accidentally killed by a sentry from the 506th…

Colonel Allen led his companies into the attack at dawn on 8th June, crossing the lines of the 2/501st towards Hell's Corner to the north of Carentan and up to the first bridges on the RN 13, at Purple Heart Lane. The Germans blew up the bridges and the 401st was pinned down by German machine-guns. They spent the night in St-Côme-du-Mont and, on the morning of 9th June, were attached to the 327th GIR.

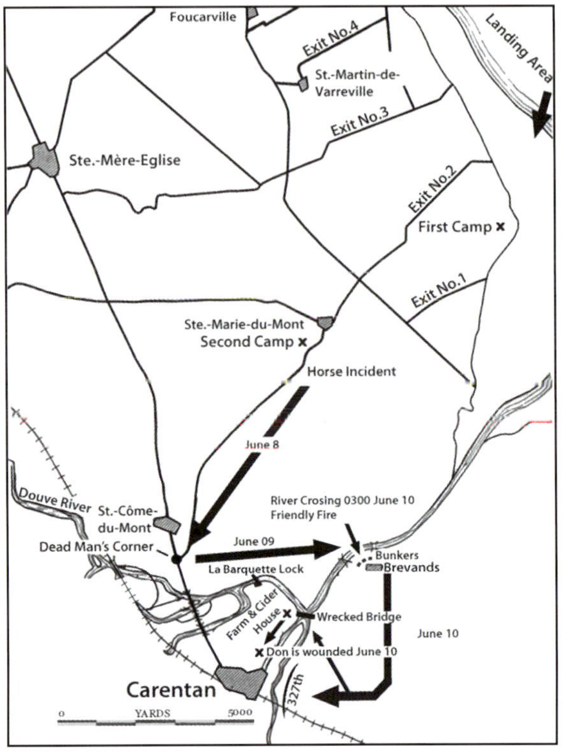

Route of the 327th GIR and its attached Third Battalion from the 401st GIR, from Utah Beach to Carentan.

George Wear had been in command of the 327th since its activation as a glider regiment. When the 101st AB was activated, the lack of qualified colonels forced Generals Lee and Bradley to retain them. Wear would suffer a major setback when his regiment was designated to travel to Normandy by sea instead of by air, due to the lack of gliders. But from the very beginning, his lack of leadership appalled his battalion commanders. On 10 June , after crossing the Douve at Brévands, the 327th was ordered to attack Carentan. This first assault failed miserably and General Taylor relieved Wear of his command, replacing him with Bud Harper, the former 401st GIR CO. (US Army)

A badge similar to the parachute insignia was authorized on 2 June 1944. These relatively small badges were placed for better visibility on a cloth background called an "oval" featuring the colors of the given regiment. This is the 327th oval. (Private collection)

Lieutenant Colonel Joseph "Bud" Harper, CO 327th Glider Infantry, 101st Airborne

Lt. Colonel Joseph H. "Bud" Harper was a career officer in charge of a battalion in the 326th Regiment of the 82nd Infantry Division in early 1942. When the 82nd became Airborne, in August 1942, he was given the new 401st Glider Infantry Regiment, with Lt. Col. Henry Leveck as Executive Officer. The 327th was the "in-house" Glider regiment in the 101st, with Colonel George Wear as Commanding Officer, and Lt. Col. Curtis Renfro as XO. Harper did his utmost to ensure his regiment was equally ranked with the 325th, 326th and 327th GIR. In late December 1943, faced with the need to increase the numbers in the para and glider regiments, his regiment was broken up, which for him was an outrage.

"Bud" Harper was literally stunned by the announcement that his beloved 401st GIR was to be broken up to strengthen the 327th and 325th GIR. The first battalion of the 401st remained with the 101st to become the 3/327th GIR, while the 2/401st left for the 82nd to become the 3/325th. There were 3179 men in the 327th GIR for Normandy. To add insult to injury, he was informed that there would no room for him in the invasion, and that he would stay behind in England. In fact, he was appointed Beachmaster to manage the arrival of the gliders in Utah on 6th June. Deeply upset, Harper called Van Horn Moseley, the CO of the 502 PIR and explained to him that he wished to take part in the invasion in one way or another and that he wanted to jump over Normandy. Moseley called a drill sergeant and gave him Harper to teach him the rudiments of jumping. The sergeant got Harper to climb onto a table, showed him how to raise his arms to hold the cords, how to jump and land in a ball. Harper did this four or five times and the sergeant said that he was ready to jump!

A few days later, an RAF plane was requisitioned to enable Harper to carry out his first jump. Harper confessed that he did not get a wink of sleep during the night before the jump, as he was scared stiff. On a cold April morning in 1944, he made his way to the aerodrome, where a jeering crew were waiting. Seeing how nervous he was, the pilot made a bet with his crew that Harper would freeze at the doorway and refuse to jump. The plane took off with Harper as the only passenger. The sergeant attached the static line and asked him to make his way towards the door. Without the slightest hesitation, Harper jumped into the void to the astonishment of the British crew. Harper landed like a feather, did a second jump and got Taylor to authorize him to jump in Normandy.

On 10th June, Colonel George S. Wear's 327th GIR had to carry out a decisive attack to take Carentan, by crossing the Douve towards Brévands. This attack got completely bogged down. Max Taylor, CO of the 101st, relieved Wear of his command. It would appear that he was to be the scapegoat for the losses suffered by the C/327th on the night of 9th-10th June. They were decimated by friendly fire, while attempting to cross the Douve. Wear is alleged not to have stuck to schedule and by crossing too soon, the glidermen in C, but also B/327th fell under friendly fire... What is certain is that the movement of the 327th from St-Côme-du-Mont was very poorly organized with battalions and companies all mixed up in an unholy mess, which certainly angered McAuliffe, who was in charge of the operation to the east of Carentan. Taylor handed over the 327th to Bud Harper. The latter took Rouzie as XO, while Renfro became G-3 in the 101st. Harper was very much liked by his men, who nicknamed him 'Dig'em deeper', which showed how attached Harper was to the safety of his men at the front. At 02:00 hrs on 10th June, Harper would move his battalions to the edge of Carentan from St Hilaire-Petitville. He would go on the attack from the wet dock at 05:00 hrs on 12 June and link up with members of the 2/506th in Carentan around the railroad station.

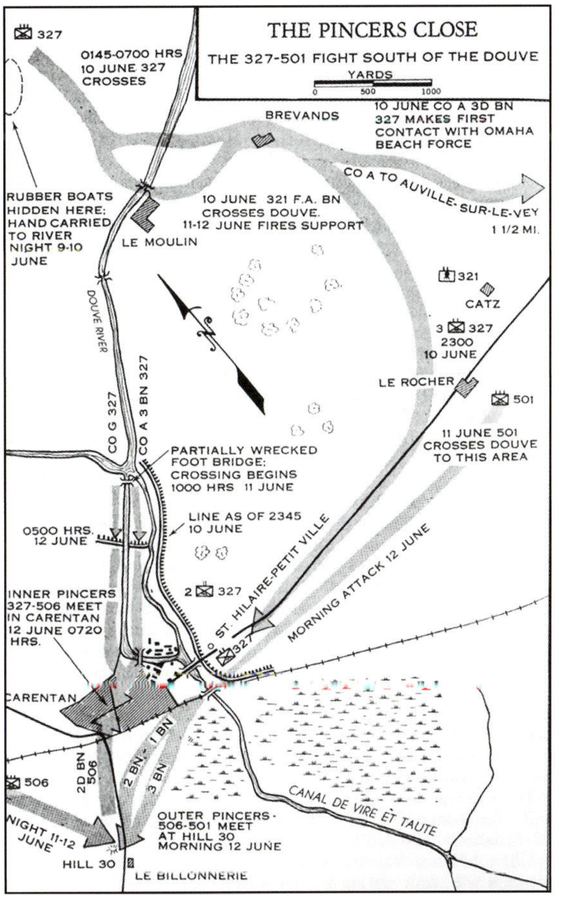

The 327th would make the decisive breakthrough and entered Carentan from both sides of the wet dock.

Joseph Harper was a tall man and wore glasses that made him look like a school teacher. At 42 years of age, he was a perfect athlete with amazing physical condition. Born in Maryland, Harper held a degree in agriculture from the University of Delaware. He went to ROTC and served in many different posts. His time came on 10 June 1944. He would lead the 401st and the 327th through the Normandy, Holland, Bastogne and Germany campaigns.

Private First Class Donald J. Rich, G/327th Glider Infantry, 101st Airborne

Don Rich, from Wayland, Iowa, a bazooka man from the G/327th, the first person to liberate Carentan.

Don was drafted in February 1943 at the age of 19 and joined the US Army at Camp Dodge near Des Moines. He trained at Camp Roberts in California, and was then sent to Bragg, where he became the bazooka man in G Company of the 327th Glider Infantry Regiment. He would go ashore on Utah Beach with most of the 101st Airborne on the afternoon of 6 June.

Don Rich, while he was not the first soldier from the 101st Airborne to enter Carentan, was certainly one of the first to liberate the town. At dawn on 11th June, he was on the edge of the wet dock. He crossed the small bridge, which had been half-demolished, to get to the western side of the dock with his bazooka on his shoulder. Bud Harper was there and told him to test the German defenses to the west of the wet dock. This is his story.

"Looking towards the south, I could see that the western part of the canal had a high dike covered with a row of trees all the way to Carentan. We were 250 yards along this dike with Frank Delarosa leading the way watching out for the slightest sign of the enemy. I was on maximum alert and rather worried, as we gradually moved along. It was hard to make out what lay ahead of us because of the trees and bushes. We went 50 yards further and then decided to head back to report to Captain Evans (G Company CO). On the way back, I saw a small single storey house to the west of the canal with a small orchard as a garden. Taking things very cautiously, we entered the house. It was full of bottles of cider. Damn! That cider was good!

We made our way back to the bridge which was reinforced by the Engineers, with boards down to make it easier to cross. We made our report to Evans (Lt Hugh Robert Evans, CO of the G/327th). Colonel Harper was also there. Delarosa declared: "No sign of the enemy, Sir". I added: "We didn't see anyone… but the cider is great!" Harper gave me a strange look: "Apple cider?" "Yes Sir" said Delarosa, "over there." Harper and Evans made their way to the house and came out with huge smiles on their faces."

Combat Infantrymen, Don Rich and Kevin Brooks.

Don was wounded in the left leg by machine gun fire during the charge led by G Company a few hours later. Delarosa was killed.

Aerial view of the wet dock .In red circle is the house where Don Rich is said to have received help from French civilians after being wounded.

Wounded during the attack along the wet dock, Don Rich bears testimony to the tough fighting encountered in the eastern sector of Carentan. (Kevin Brooks)

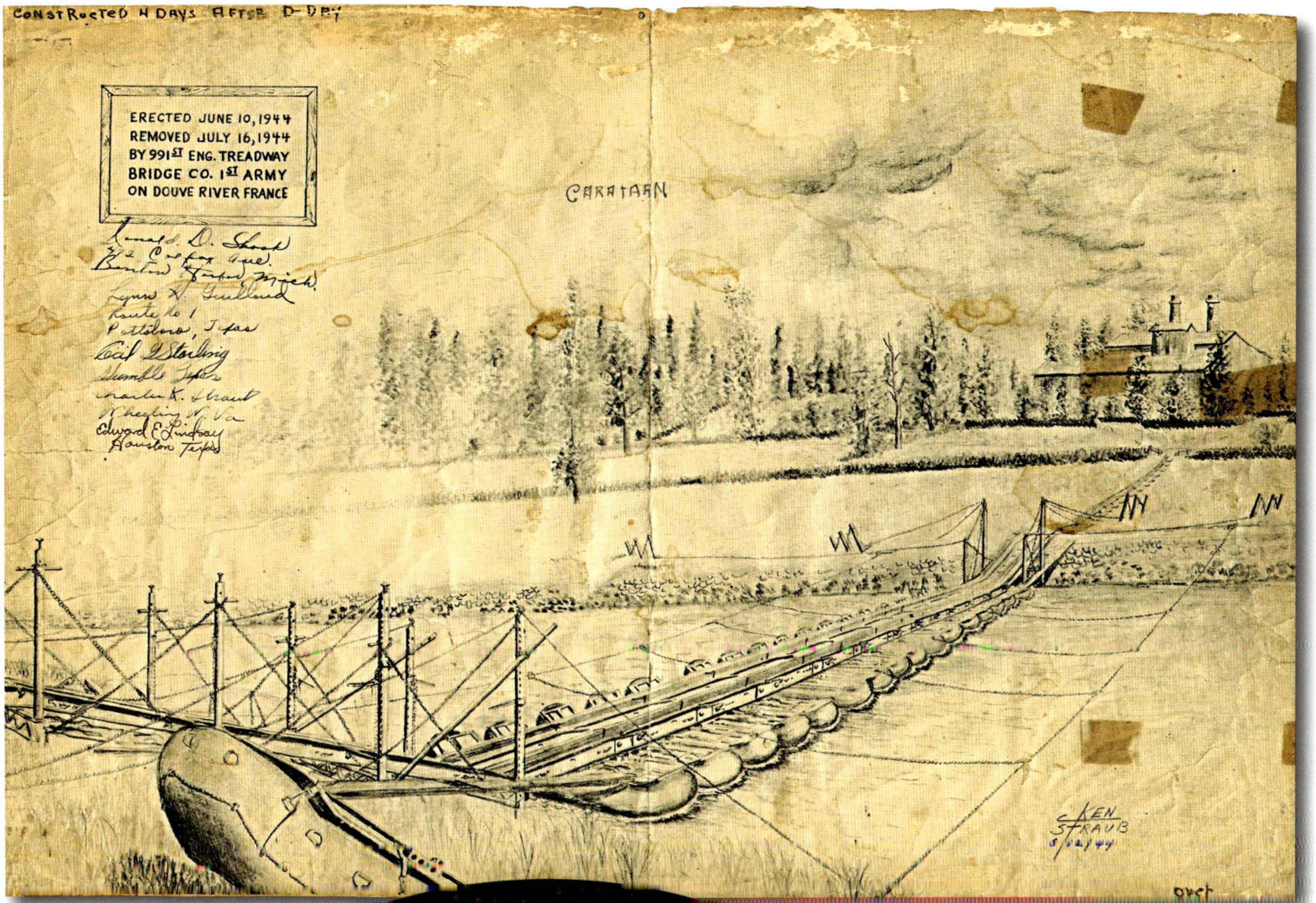

Above: in order to replace the two wooden bridges built by the Germans at Le Port in Brévands, destroyed by US Airplanes on 7 June, the 991st Engineers established a pontoon bridge on 9 June, to be used by the 327th and the 501st in the Douve crossing on 10 June.

Left: helmet bearing the tactical sign of the 1/327th. (Collection Michel Quiliez)

Above: on 15 August 1942, the 327th Infantry Regiment was still an organic part of the glorious 82nd Infantry Division. The next day, the Division became Airborne, and the 327th became a glider regiment and the organic regiment of the newly activated 101st Airborne Division.

Below: November 1942; George Wear shows up at the E and G Companies, 327th Thanksgiving dinner. Most soldiers still do not wear the Airborne tab.

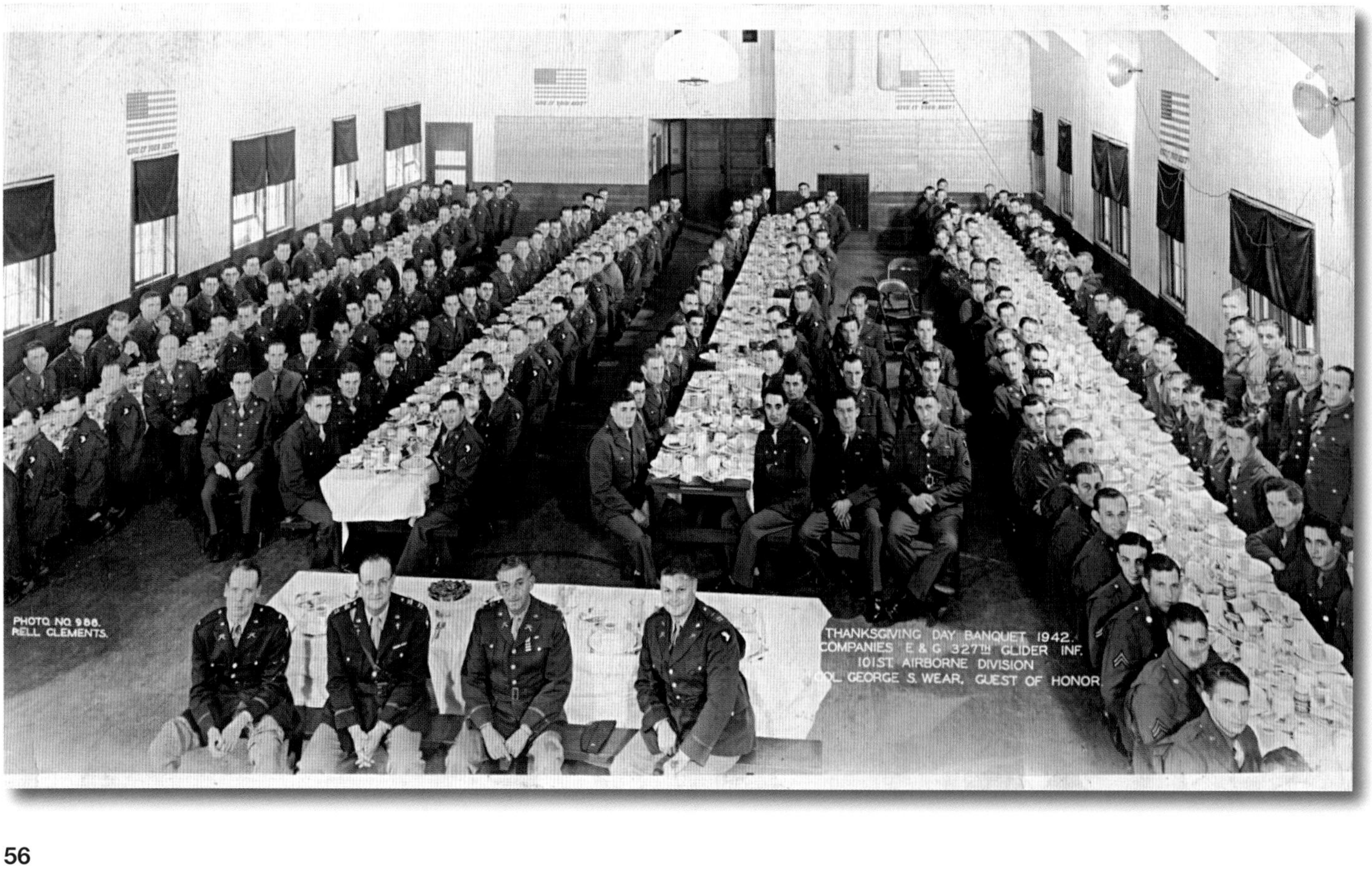

Pulitzer Prize winner, Louis Aston Marantz Simpson, G/327th, 101st Airborne

Louis was born on 27th March 1923 in Kingston, Jamaica. His father was black and a British citizen. Louis also had British nationality. His mother, Rosalind Marantz was a Russian actress, who had emigrated to the U.S.A. looking for work in the film industry, where she was hired as a costume assistant for the actress Annette Kellerman, and sent to Jamaica where filming was taking place. Louis was a very smart as a boy and was accepted by Columbia University in New York. However, he interrupted his studies to sign up for the Army. He was initially in tanks before joining the 101st Airborne and their Glider regiment. He would serve in all the Division's campaigns in Normandy, Holland, Belgium and Germany. He was wounded on the morning of 12 June during the attack near the wet dock in Carentan. At that particular moment, he was the runner for Captain Evans, G Company CO. After the war, Louis returned to Paris to study French culture and civilization at the Sorbonne. One night In Paris, he dreamed he was marching with his company alongside a tree-lined dock. Suddenly, shells and bullets rained down around him. Someone was shouting nearby in Italian. He woke up and wrote a poem entitled "Carentan O Carentan." This poem was set to music by the French composer, Aubert Lemeland, as well as by the musician, Benjamin Lees.

Pictures of Lou Simpson are scarce. He is seen here, 4th from the right, next to his company commander, Captain Hugh Evans, in Holland. Lou was WIA in Carentan.

7. Objective, Brévands

The third battalion of the 506th Parachute Infantry Regiment took off at 23:30 hrs (Double British Summer Time) on Monday 5 June 1944 from Exeter aerodrome, Devon. More than a battalion, this was a real Combat Team, including 630 men and 50 officers from HQ, G, H and I Companies, who were joined by 43 Engineers from C Company of the 326th AEB, 3 artillerymen from the Navy and 3 artillery observers, 6 medical officers, 4 counter-intelligence agents, and 26 demolition specialists from the Regiment Headquarters Company that Lt. Col. Wolverton led into battle. Dropped before the biggest invasion in history into the salt marshes in Normandy, these paratroopers were aiming for two highly strategic bridges spanning the Douve. For many these would be a case of a bridge too far…

It was at 23:48 hrs (British time) that Lieutenant Colonel Frank X. Krebs, commander of the 440th TCG took off from Exeter aboard his Gooney Bird N° 292717, Stoy Hora, which transported Lt. Colonel Robert Wolverton, stick commander. 44 planes from the 95th, 96th, 97th and 98th Troop carrier squadrons followed. After an incident-free Channel crossing and distant Flak over the peninsula, Krebs picked up the signal from the Pathfinders. At 01:36 hrs, he gave the troopers the long-awaited signal, "stand up and hook up!" Four minutes later, the green light came on in the plane and, in tight formation, Wolverton and his men jumped into the unknown.

In the original plan that had been long debated at headquarters, the 3rd Battalion 506, along with the 1st and 2nd Battalions of the 501st PIR, were scheduled to be dropped over Drop Zone "D" to the south of Vierville and to the east of Angoville-au-Plain. This DZ offered a huge wide open space measuring over half a mile wide and one and a half miles long, split in the middle by a small canal in the marshes close to the small village of Angoville. In the distance, there was the town of Carentan. This, the widest DZ, was due to serve as the emergency drop zone perimeter for any aircraft from the 101st that found itself in difficulty. The two bat-

The place known as Le Port at Brévands. One can make out the footbridge. (US Army)

On this aerial photo, what remains of the road bridge below left can be seen bottom, left and the footbridge built by the Germans over the Douve in 1943. Not hearing from his Third Battalion, Robert Sink, CO 506th PIR, fearing that the bridge was still in German hands, called on the US Air Force to destroy the bridges. Three Mustang P.51 aircraft from the 353rd Fighter Group and four P.47 Thunderbolts attacked and destroyed the bridges, despite all the efforts from the paratroopers to signal their presence at the bridges. (US Army)

talions from the 501st PIR, so precious to their fiery commander, Colonel Howard R Johnson, came together in two Serials, N° 14 and 15, (name used by IX TCC – publisher's note) or, in other words, 1,475 men, and were to deal with the locks at La Barquette and two bridges on the N13 road to Carentan. These two Serials had taken off from Merryfield just before the 3/506 in order to be dropped before Wolverton's men.

The latter were aiming for two bridges built by the Germans near Le Port on the Douve, and the small ferry which crossed the river at this point. The first of the two bridges, the closest to the sea at the place called Le Moulin, was a wooden foot bridge built in late 1942 located 250 yards downstream of the ferry. The second objective was a road bridge that the Germans had built between August and December 1943 to make it easier for vehicles to go between the Calvados department and the Cotentin peninsula, between what the Allies would call Omaha and Utah Beach. This road bridge was located 750 yards upstream of the ferry, towards Carentan, at the level of the Fortin family's farm.

The plan of action for the Third Battalion was to assemble in DZ 'D' when the company bugler, Pfc Don C. Ross, sounded his horn and then rush towards the two bridges to take them intact. Then, they would cross the Douve and set up a bridgehead to the south of the river occupying the heights near Brévands, while awaiting the arrival of the troops that were coming ashore on Omaha Beach. Two platoons of the C/326th Airborne Engineer Battalion reinforced the battalion in order to help the demolition experts from RHQ 3/506 to mine the bridge and prevent the Germans from accessing it, if the establishment of a bridgehead turned out to be impossible.

The ferry crossing, opposite the Brévands phosphate factory, was the third passage over the Douve that had to be secured or destroyed by the 3/506th by the evening of D-Day.

Upstream from Brévands, close to Carentan, the road bridge and the "German road" leading to Utah Beach.

Chambliss's G company at Bragg in 1943. (US Army)

For D-Day, out of affection and respect for their leader, Turner Chambliss, the Second Platoon of G Company, wore names tags with the inked words West Point on them. Chambliss, a true West Pointer, noticed it upon boarding and showed no reaction. As he was dying in the arms of a H Company sergeant along the Douve, he wondered why his men wrote West Point on their jump suits, fearing it was out of mockery. He did not realize how much his men were fond of him...

First Lieutenant Turner M. Chambliss, West Point 1943

Turner Mason Chambliss Jr. (15 July 1921 – 6 June 1944) was a typical West Pointer, an idealist who was harsh, but fair with his men. The son and grandson of a soldier, he spent his life in army posts, Benning, Washington, Hawaii...He entered West Point on 1st July 1939 and graduated from the academy in January 1943, after hesitating between aviation and the infantry. He excelled in athletics and swimming. Between his first and second year at the "Point", he took flying lessons in Ulvade in Texas, but did not complete his training. He wanted to follow in the footsteps of his father and attend the Benning Infantry School after West Point. It was there that he discovered Jump school. He trained with the paratroopers from 5th May to 5th June 1943. He became fascinated by the Airborne, and asked to join a parachute unit. He was appointed to the 506th PIR during the Tennessee Maneuvers in the summer of 1943. He wrote to his father: "*I don't know why the paratroopers receive extra pay; jumping is so much fun!*" He arrived in Ramsbury with G/506, and spent there, in his own words, "*the finest moments of my life with a gang of paratroopers,*" as First Lieutenant, Platoon Leader, Second Platoon, Company G, 506th Parachute Infantry Regiment, 101st Airborne Division. He took off from Exeter on 5th June after 23:00 hrs BDST and landed not far from St-Côme-du-Mont. In his pocket he had an aerial photograph of the target and was able to make his way towards the bridges at Brévands. Just before sunrise on 6 June 1944, two small groups, one led by Captain Charles Shettle, staff officer of the 3/506, and Chambliss, reached the bridges at Brévands, with Shettle going to the footbridge and Chambliss the road bridge at 05:00 hrs with nine men. With their respective groups, they began the battle. 69 troopers in all, would prevent the Germans from crossing the Douve for three days. Chambliss would be among the KIA. Six foot four, he towered over the embankments along the Douve, with his silhouette standing out in the morning light. He was hit in the throat by two sniper bullets. It was 07:30 hrs on 6th June 1944.

Frederick Bahlau, H/506th Parachute Infantry, 101st Airborne, two Silver Stars

Fred was one of the major heroes in the liberation of Carentan. Supply Sergeant with H Company of the 506th Parachute Regiment attached to the 101st Airborne, his actions at the bridges at Brévands on 7 June 1944 saw him awarded the greatest distinction for the American army, the Silver Star. On 20th June 1944, General Troy Middleton, commander of the American VIIIth Corps awarded him his medal at one of the three famous ceremonies held on the Place de la République in Carentan.

Fred Bahlau was born on 30 August 1923 in Jackson, Michigan. Of German origin, his grandfather had been a soldier in the Imperial Army before the First World War. As soon as Pearl Harbor was attacked, he tried to sign up, but was not yet 18 and his parents refused to sign a waiver. He waited until his nineteenth birthday before signing up in Detroit on 23rd September 1942. A recruiting officer helped him fill in his application to convince his mother that he was only signing up to train as an electrician. He arrived at Fort Benning and volunteered for the paratroops. He quickly became corporal, then Staff Sergeant in the Service Company in the 506th PIR, assigned to H Company.

He was Supply Sergeant in H Company, when he jumped over Normandy on the night of 6 June

1944. The work required a lot of cunning and resourcefulness and Bahlau was known for his ability to get his hands on whatever his company needed by any means possible. He landed on the wrong side of the Douve, towards Brévands, but managed to rejoin the surviving men from the 3rd battalion, which was decimated on the Drop Zone to the south of Angoville-au-Plain. He placed himself under the command of Captain Charles Shettle, S-3 (Plans and Operations) of the battalion. Shettle ordered him to take 5 or 6 men across the Douve again, using one of the two bridges built by the Germans, in order to test the German defenses to the south of the Douve, and to attempt to set up a bridgehead there if possible. In the company of Don Zahn, Hank Di Carlo, George Montilio and Sergeant Harry Clawson, he crossed the Douve at the level of the road bridge upstream from Brévands and immediately came under German machine gun fire. Fred was the fourth man to try to cross the bridge under enemy fire. Hank Di Carlo was hit in the chest. Fred tried to kill the German who had fired, but his Thompson machine-gun, which was full of sand, jammed. It was Don Zahn, who killed the German. Fred dragged Di Carlo into the shelter of the parapet and gave him first aid. He then headed for the right bank of the Douve, which he inspected for 500 yards or so. His presence along with that of his fellow soldiers blocked a German counter-attack that attempted to grab the two bridges near Brévands, the footbridge and road bridge. Fred returned four hours later and brought Di Carlo back towards the American lines and the aid post set up at the Fortin farm in Pénême. His feats at the bridges at Brévands on 7 June were honored when he was awarded his first Silver Star.

On 13 June, during the terrible battle at Bloody Gulch to the south of Carentan, facing a counter-attack from the 17. SS-Panzergrenadier-Division, he was appointed First Sergeant of H/506th, after Sergeant Gordon Bolles was seriously wounded. In a U.S. infantry company, the First Sergeant was part of the relay between the rank and file troopers and the officers. When the latter came out of hospital in England in July, H Company found itself with two First Sergeants. Fred was therefore transferred to HQ Company in the 3/506th as their new First Sergeant. He would keep this role in Holland and at Bastogne. It was near Opheusden on 5th October 1944 that Fred got his second Silver Star, when he went

Fed Bahlau, from staff sergeant to lieutenant, an officer and a gentleman. (Mark Bando)

under enemy fire to recover some important documents left by Major Harwick in a jeep by the Linge Canal after an ambush. After Bastogne, Fred received a Battlefield Commission, a promotion obtained on the battlefield and was made 2nd Lieutenant. A month later, he became First Lieutenant.

He returned to Onsted, Michigan at the end of the war, married his high school sweetheart and took over his father's electrical firm. He became President of the Irish Hills Tourist Association and created the Electric Maintenance and Repair Company in Jackson, Michigan. Frederick A. Bahlau died on Tuesday 21 October, 2014 at the age of 91 in Toledo, Ohio.

Above: Fred received his first Silver Star in Carentan, on 20 June in the Place de la République. Madame Evelyne Le Gouix congratulates him. They would meet again 50 years later!

Below: After his daring patrol south of the Douve, Bahlau poses in his foxhole along the northern bank of the river. (Coll. Mark Bando)

Lt Charles Santarsiero, I/506th Parachute Infantry, 101st Airborne Division, hero of Brévands

Lieutenant Charles "Sandy" Santarsiero from Scranton, Pennsylvania, was one of the few representatives of I Company from the 506th PIR close to the road bridge in Brévands. On 8 June, he earned a DSC after wiping out a company of Germans.

On Thursday 8 June, Santarsiero was observing the area ahead of his position on the banks of the Douve with his binoculars, looking for friendly troops marching up from the eastern coast of the Cotentin peninsula. But instead, he caught sight of several companies of German soldiers retreating from Utah Beach towards the bridges at Brévands. They did not seem to be aware of the American presence in the sector. Santarsiero alerted his men and told them to stay hidden until the Germans were within 70 yards. When he ordered them to open fire, it was a complete surprise. Most of the German soldiers leading their companies were struck down and those behind ran off into a large field surrounded by high hedges. Santarsiero decided to attack the Germans before they had time to reassemble to counter-attack. He left Lieutenant Linton Barling (KIA in Holland) the responsibility of defending the bridge and ran towards the nearest hedge. He found a fully prepared position there that had been abandoned by some troopers. It was a very long v-shaped trench pointing towards the hedge. Less than 40 yards away, Santarsiero could see the German officers screaming their orders at a group of soldiers. He could see six American prisoners among the group, who were carrying stretchers. Santarsiero opened fire on the Germans, killing several of them. The prisoners carrying the stretchers ran off in every direction, dragging the stretchers with them. Santarsiero would never see them again.

A German MG 42 opened fire on Santarsiero's position, covering him with dust and shards of rock. Then, for some unknown reason, they suddenly stopped firing.

In groups of ten, the panicking Germans scattered in every direction ahead of Santarsiero. He fired on the rear of the group and gradually moved up through the column. Then, another group appeared in his firing range, and Santarsiero carried out the same movement in the opposite direction. He caused a huge number of victims, until he had no more targets. (Santarsiero had been a shooting instructor at the Infantry School at Fort Benning). He would later explain that he used a Garand M-1 during this action and used up an entire ammunition pouch. By firing so rapidly at a distance of less than 100 yards, almost all of the bullets hit their target.

Three Germans waving a white flag then appeared. Santarsiero came out of his hole and walked towards them. He began to offer help to the most severely injured. Soon, the whole field was full of injured Germans all wanting to surrender. Santarsiero indicated the position of Captain Shettle further along the embankment on the northern banks of the Douve. He then heard the word "*Kamerad*" coming from his right. It came from those who had been using the MG 42 and had been firing on him just a few moments before. The machine-gun, which was fully loaded, was pointed straight at him. Luck was on his side, as it would have been very easy for the Germans to cut him in half. Instead of that, they remained hidden watching their comrades surrender, before they too surrendered. These prisoners were sent to join other German prisoners taken near the footbridge. Santarsiero entrusted the MG 42 machine-gun to those defending the bridge, who were glad of the extra fire power.

Nineteen officers and 117 soldiers from Shettle's 3/506th Battalion survived and reached Hiesville after the battles around Brévands. During the three days of fighting for the bridges, they lost seven men and 21 were injured. In 'Rendez Vous with Destiny', Rapport and Northwood say the battalion claimed a total of 60 to 70 German killed or wounded, and 258 prisoners. Of these 258 POWs, Santarsiero claims to have captured 179 during his actions on 8 June. Santarsiero, nicknamed 'Sandy', was also referred to as 'The blue goose,' by his comrades. Sandy had been very sick during the Atlantic crossing aboard the Samaria, to the point where his skin had turned a shade of blue…

Charles Santarsiero. Sandy used to belong to C Company, 1/506th PIR. But his commanding officer, Lt. Colonel Billy Turner (KIA in Beaumont), a true Southerner, hated all Yankees. Sandy got transferred to Item Company, 3/506th shortly before D-Day. (Mark Bando)

Major George Grant, Battalion XO, killed on 6 June just like his CO, Bob Wolverton. George was related to the former President of the United States, Ulysses Grant.

Opposite: Charles Shettle at the end of the war.

Below: 3/506th officers at Littlecote Manor in England, where the battalion and the Regimental Headquarters personnel were billeted. Major Grant leads the parade, followed by James "Jeb" Holstun, also KIA, Charles Shettle and Lieutenants Morgan and King.

Captain Charles Gordon Shettle, 3/506th PIR, 101st Airborne

Of the 575 officers and men in the 3/506 who jumped over Normandy in Drop Zone D, 103 were killed, including Lieutenant Colonel Robert L. Wolverton, their Executive Officer (XO) George Grant, and Captain Harold Van Antwerp, the Commander of G Company. First Lieutenant James D. Holstun, the Battalion's S-1, died late on 6 June on reaching the Douve. 75 troopers were captured, including Captain Robert Harwick, commander of H Company and Captain John McKnight, Commander of I Company, former assistant to Wolverton in HQ 3/506. Captain Harwick managed to escape and took the command of the Battalion on 9 June. Incidentally, Harwick was once again asked to take the command of a battalion replacing a CO KIA on 18 December in Noville near Bastogne, as he took over the 1/506 after the death of Lt Col. James Laprade.

At dawn on 6 June, Captain Charles Gordon Shettle (the Battalion's S-3) was walking towards Les Droueries and found two officers and twelve men. He decided to head towards his battalion's objective, the Brévands bridges over the Douve. On the way, he picked up sixteen men and two more officers. One of them was a guy from the C/326th Airborne Engineer Battalion with a Mohawk haircut, who dynamited (C2) an electrical sub-station. Around twenty men joined Shettle and so it was with around sixty troopers that he reached the Brévands road bridge, upstream of the place known as Le Port. His arrival caused several Germans, who were hiding out on the right bank of the Douve, to flee. A sniper shot 1st Lt Turner Chambliss in the throat. As he was so tall, he could be seen above the river embankment. Five men crossed the Douve using the superstructure of the bridge. They destroyed three concealed machine-gun nests before withdrawing to the left bank. The bridge was then set with explosives to prepare its possible destruction. Shettle and his little group, which was growing in size with the arrival of troopers who had lost their way, remained in these positions throughout the day and the following night. On June, with no news of his 3rd battalion, Colonel Robert F. Sink, commander of the 506th PIR, believing that the bridges were still in enemy hands, ordered their destruction. During two American P-47 and P-51 fighter-bomber missions the bridges were attacked and destroyed. From 6th to 8th June, the reduced numbers left in the 3/506 PIR, 117 men and 19 officers, managed to ward off German attacks, taking 258 prisoners and killing between sixty and seventy. The 3/506 PIR was relieved on the evening of the 8 June by the 327th Glider Infantry. The mission would finally be accomplished with just 150 men, while it had been planned to use more than 700. During the battle for the bridges, the 3/506th suffered seven dead and 21 wounded. For their courage and heroic behavior in Brévands, four men from the Battalion received the Distinguished Service Cross (D.S.C.): Lieutenant Charles Santarsiero from I Company, Sergeant George Montilio from H Company H, Pfc. Donald Zahn from H Company, and Pfc. Andrew Sosnak from the medical detachment.

Don Zahn with Al Hassenzahl, C/506th Commanding Officer, recipient of 4 Purple Hearts and one Silver Star. (Mark Bando)

Airborne Command Shoulder Patch Insignia; the 501st and the 506th, prior to being attached to the 101st were under the Airborne Command administration. (Private Collection)

Donald Eugene Zahn, H Company, 506th Parachute Infantry, 101st Airborne, DSC in Brévands

Born on 15 October, 1920, in Bellingham, Minnesota, Donald Eugene Zahn, died on 15 May 2016. He was covered in glory from the first hours of the landings on 6 June 1944 for his actions near Brévands. An only son, he left school in 1939 and went to the University of Minnesota, where he excelled in athletics and American football. He signed up as a volunteer joining H Company, 1st platoon of the 506th Parachute Infantry Regiment from his training in Toccoa in 1942. He was injured twice during training and was moved out of the mortar squad to become a scout. On 6 June, he was one of the first members of the 3rd Battalion of the 506th PIR to reach the objective, the Brévands bridges over the Douve, with only Lieutenant Ken Christianson and Pfcs Sam Porter and Don Arminio ahead of him. At around 05:30 hrs, a group of around forty men under the command of Captain Charles Shettle, the Regiment's S-3, reached Brévands. Shettle asked for volunteers to cross the road bridge upstream from the place known as Les Moulins in Brévands, to test and evaluate German defenses. Zahn, who was just a Private First Class, raised his hand. Shettle sent Private First Class Hank Di Carlo, Arminio, Sergeant George Montillio and Staff Sergeant Fred Bahlau with him. Don Zahn was the first to cross the bridge and reach the enemy bank. Now in enemy territory, Di Carlo was seriously wounded by German pistol fire. Zahn shot the German with his Thompson. The Germans were dangerously close to the small group and Di Carlo was helped onto a beam to allow him to get back across the Douve. Zahn, Bahlau, Arminio and Montillio tried to cover him with their guns. They got back to the left bank of the Douve and remained in position until reinforcements arrived on 8 June. A little later, close to Fortin farm in Pénême, around fifteen

Donald Zahn refused to shoot prisoners of war in Normandy.

Luger picked up by Zahn during his patrol south of the Douve at Brévands. (Photo Mark Bando)

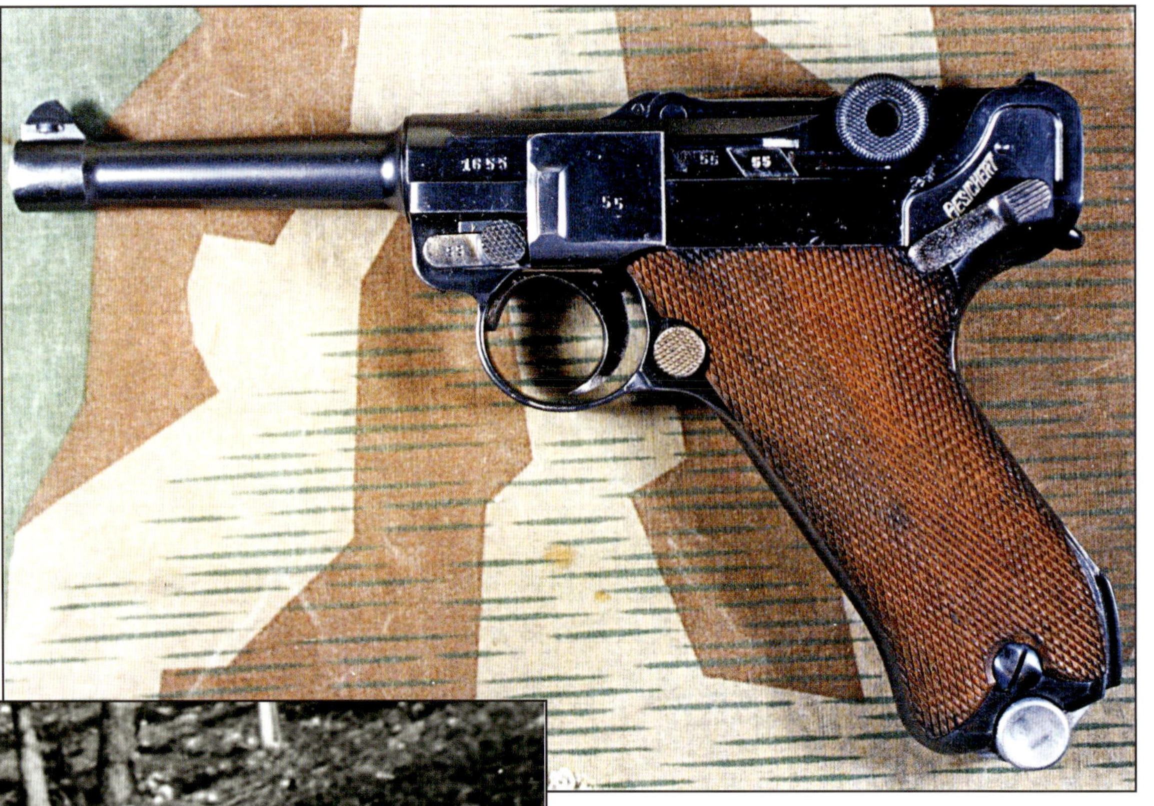

Don Zahn in Austria at the end of the war.

Ukrainian volunteers from *Ost Bataillon 439* were taken prisoner as they attempted to retreat towards the Douve. Captain Shettle, realizing that he did not have enough men to look after them and as laid down in orders before the invasion, told Don Zahn to eliminate them. Don refused, suggesting that they should be kept alive to be questioned. Shettle accepted, and Don was later able to say: *"I'm pleased to have saved some lives."* (1) Don was awarded the Distinguished Service Cross for his action in Brévands. In December 1944, he was promoted to the rank of 2nd Lieutenant, and ended the war in Berchtesgaden, in charge of looking after Hitler's eagle's nest with the rank of 1st Lieutenant, 2nd Platoon, C/506th.

Don Zahn eventually received his Distinguished Service Cross for his actions at Brévands in 1945 at… Berchtesgaden. (Private collection)

(1) This was only a reprieve for the Ukranians as the USA handed over the "Eastern volunteers" to Stalin according to the agreement made at the Yalta Conference. (Publisher's note)

Harry Clawson and his pal Fred Bahlau, both Silver Star recipients in Carentan on 20 June 1944.

Harry Clawson, H/506th Parachute Infantry, 101st Airborne. A dangerous game

Harry could turn his hand to anything and was scared by nothing; the perfect paratrooper. From a young age, he wandered around the countryside with his 22 Long Rifle, drinking water from the springs and feeding himself by hunting. A real death dodger, he organized races with his brother aboard petrol tankers belonging to the fuel company for which he worked. The Airborne was exactly what he was looking for. In Normandy, he would earn himself a Silver Star in the battles around Brévands. It was there that he began to collect military medals from the German prisoners or corpses that he would pin inside his jumpsuit. His friend, Fred Bahlau from H 506 warned him on several occasions that if the Germans got hold of him with these medals, he was a dead man. But Harry, a real Dare Devil, could not see the danger. On 5th October 1944 in Opheusden in the Netherlands, Harry was posted on the second floor of a house near the railroad station, with an observation mission for the mortar squad. The Germans spotted him and opened fire. Wounded in the eyes, he was taken prisoner. When the Germans tried to take care of him, they discovered his collection of medals inside his jacket. They took him outside and executed him without any sort of trial. He was declared Missing In Action until 1971. He was also awarded the Bronze Star.

On the day after receiving his Silver Star in Carentan on 20th June, he was threatened with a court martial for not wearing the regulation tie in public.

Harry Clawson would fall victim to his hunger for war souvenirs...

Allied prisoners of war at the Saint-Lô military horse stables. Six of these men belong to RHQ 506th, including Don Ross, the regimental bugler.

Captain John T. McKnight: A 77-pound American football star

It is well known how much the 3rd battalion of the 506th Parachute Infantry Regiment suffered. On 6 June, this battalion's objective was the Brévands bridges. Flying over Saint-Côme-du-Mont, the unit, under the command of Lt. Colonel Bob Wolverton, was literally decimated, largely because of machine gun fire from the bell tower from the Church in St-Côme. Of the 575 officers and men in the 3/506 who jumped, 103 were killed, including Lieutenant Colonel Robert L. Wolverton, his Executive Officer (second in command) George Grant, and Captain Harold Van Antwerp, G Company commander. First Lieutenant James D. Holstun, the Battalion's S-1 died a little later on 6 June upon reaching the Douve. 75 troopers were taken prisoner, including Captain Robert Harwick, H Company commander and Captain John McKnight, I Company commander and former assistant to Wolverton in HQ 3/506.

Captain Harwick managed to escape and take command of the Battalion on 9 June. Incidentally, Harwick was once again asked to take the command of a battalion replacing a CO KIA on 18 December in Noville near Bastogne, as he had taken over the 1/506 after the death of Lt. Col. James Laprade.

John T. McKnight was originally from Toccoa, Georgia, the first home of the 506th PIR. In the thirties, John was a leading figure in the Georgia University football team. He was even captain of the team in his final year in 1935. He then signed up for the Army and soon reached the rank of Captain in HQ Company of the 3rd Battalion, 506th. When the Regiment arrived in England in September 1943, he was given command of Item Company. Shortly after landing, he was captured on 6 June in Saint-Côme-du-Mont. This was the start of a bitter struggle for the soldier, which only ended when the war itself came to an end, because all he could think about was escaping. For a while, he was held prisoner in Starvation Hill, the name given by captured GIs to the military equestrian center in Saint Lô, which was transformed into a prison by the Germans, who would practically deprive their prisoners of food for several days. All of his escape attempts failed and he ended the war in Stalag 3A near Berlin weighing just 77 pounds!

The equestrian centers were military establishments in charge of supplying horses for the cavalry units at the beginning of the 19th Century. These centers grew into stud farms. It was in 1826 that the Saint Lô supply center moved to the premises given to them by the stud farm behind Sainte-Croix Church.

The Germans placed the American paratroopers captured in the area there for several days, starving them, as they were only allowed a thin vegetable broth once a day...

Veterans also remember another Starvation/hungry hill. This was a convent located near Tessy-sur-Vire in Troisgots, which was also used a temporary detention center by the Germans, who applied the same diet to their prisoners as in Saint-Lô, depriving them of food.

John McKnight became a POW right after landing in Normandy. Like many others, he would endure the hardships of the *Kriegsgefangenen*, deprived of food, forced to march endless hours, often without shoes and constantly strafed by allied airplanes. This picture was taken at the military horse *Dépôt de Remonte* in Saint-Lô.

A iconic 6 June photo, in fact taken on 4 June at Exeter. Don Ross carries, under his front parachute, the bugler that was supposed to assemble his battalion in the dark.

Donald Clifton Ross: the Normandy bugle boy

Everyone has seen the series of pictures taken by and for the Signal Corps, probably on the afternoon of the 5 June 1944 at Exeter aerodrome; LTC Robert Wolverton's stick posed for a photographer and cameraman as they were given an imaginary run down of the landings. The pictures were taken in front of Stick#2 C47 #315087 plane, Lady Lillian, and not in front of the real plane, which a few hours later would take Wolverton to his death, C-47 Stick#1 #292717, Colonel Krebs's Stoy Hora, 440th Troop Carrier Squadron. In this photo report, the troopers had not yet blackened their faces and for that reason, they would all enter the history books. Their destiny was however less glamorous: Wolverton like four members of his stick, was killed in his harness before he had even touched the ground in Normandy. The others would all be taken prisoner. Most would escape on 8 June, taking advantage of their guards' hasty retreat.

The trooper seen here in this often published photo, is Pfc. Donald Clifton Ross. Don trained in Toccoa and Benning with I/506. In 1943, he became the trumpeter for HQ 3/506 and Wolverton made him his personal guard for the jump over Normandy. He jumped with the clarion that he was supposed to use to help assemble the troops on the ground. He was wounded during the jump and taken prisoner when he touched down. He went through the horrors of Starvation Hill near Saint-Lô. Ross escaped during his transfer to a stalag in Germany and ended the war in the ranks of the Czech resistance movement!

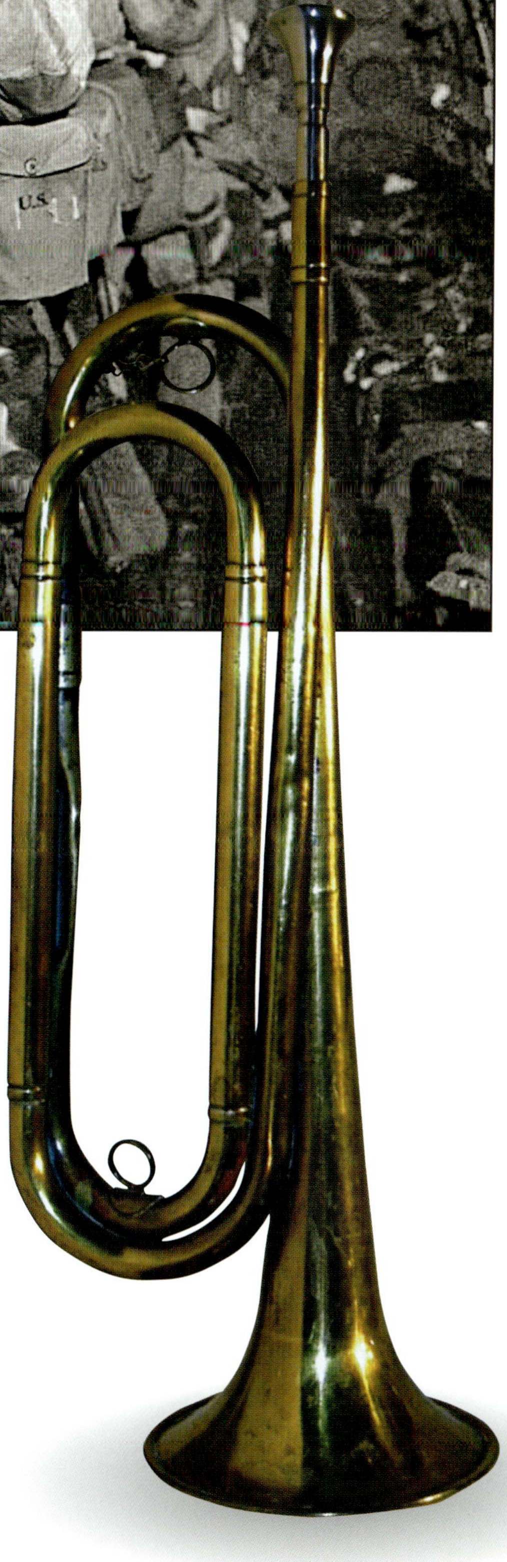

Bugler similar to the one carried by Don Ross.

8. The attack and capture of Carentan

G Company from the 2/327th GIR was attached to the 1/401st to lead the attack on Carentan from the north east. The 1/327th was kept in reserve, replaced by the 501st Parachute Infantry, which had just crossed the Douve. BG Anthony McAuliffe was in command of this Task Force. The attack began at 10:00 hrs on Sunday 11 June 1944 under the watch of Max Taylor, who was there as an observer. Under a barrage of artillery fire and German shelling, the two companies moved forward around 450 yards on either side of the wet dock , before being pinned down by the machine-guns firing from the first houses in the town.

Harper escaped death by the skin of his nose whilst moving up to the front line. The situation was a stalemate. Throughout the day, the firing continued using every weapon available in Carentan. In the evening, Harper met up with Taylor, McAuliffe (artillery from the 101st) and Howard Johnson, CO of the 501st and Courtney Hodges, 1st Army Deputy Commander, in the place known as Le Rocher. They modified the plan of attack; the 506th PIR replaced the 502nd in the attack towards Hill 30 in the south. Harper had to hold on to the wet dock with his 401st renewing the attack along the canal. Skeet Johnson's Geronimos (501st PIR) were taken out of their reserve position and crossed the Douve in Brévands to carry out a large encircling movement via the east. On 9 June, the 501st had regrouped in the Vierville sector. Johnson's men began to advance towards the south east. They crossed the Douve using a metal bridge erected by the 238th Combat Engineer Battalion. On 10 June, the Geronimos passed through Brévands and Catz and headed towards Saint-Hilaire-Petitville, where they prepared to attack Hill 30, a hillside solidly defended by many machine-gun and mortar positions. On the morning of the twelfth, the troopers set off across the marshland to the east of Hill 30 and took the objective after a furious and bloody battle. They then turned due south and faced head on the counter-attack from Fallschirmjäger-Regiment 6 *and the* 37. SS-Panzer-Grenadier-Regiment *in La Billonnerie.*

The night of the 11 to 12 June was horrible for Carentan. In addition to enemy fire, there was the American artillery and the shells from the big naval guns. Allen and his boys from the 401st understood what dig deeper meant!

At five in the morning of 12 June, Captain Eldridge Naugher's 401st jumped out of their foxholes alongside the wet dock and charged towards Carentan. They were the first to enter the town. Bob Sink in the south pushed his 2/506 into the town towards the station, which he found was only occupied by a few snipers. Running out of munitions, Major *Baron van der Heydte's* Fallschirmjäger *made their escape in the darkness. At 07:30 hrs on 12 June, the paratroopers and glidermen came together in the town. Harper, Allen, and Colonel Bob Strayer, boss of the 2/506th found themselves in a house not far from the station, where they opened a bottle of freshly liberated wine. The Germans felt by 11 June that they were threatened with being encircled. Their artillery, and a few snipers remained behind slowing down the advance of the GIs, and allowing the bulk of the* FJ. Reg 6 *forces to retreat during the night of 11 to 12 June. Only the area around the railroad station saw some bitter fighting up to the final moments.*

The Glidermen's attack on Carentan. The 327th GIR and its 3rd Battalion of 1/401st, made the decisive thrust from the east and along the wet dock, the still heavily defended Carentan marina.

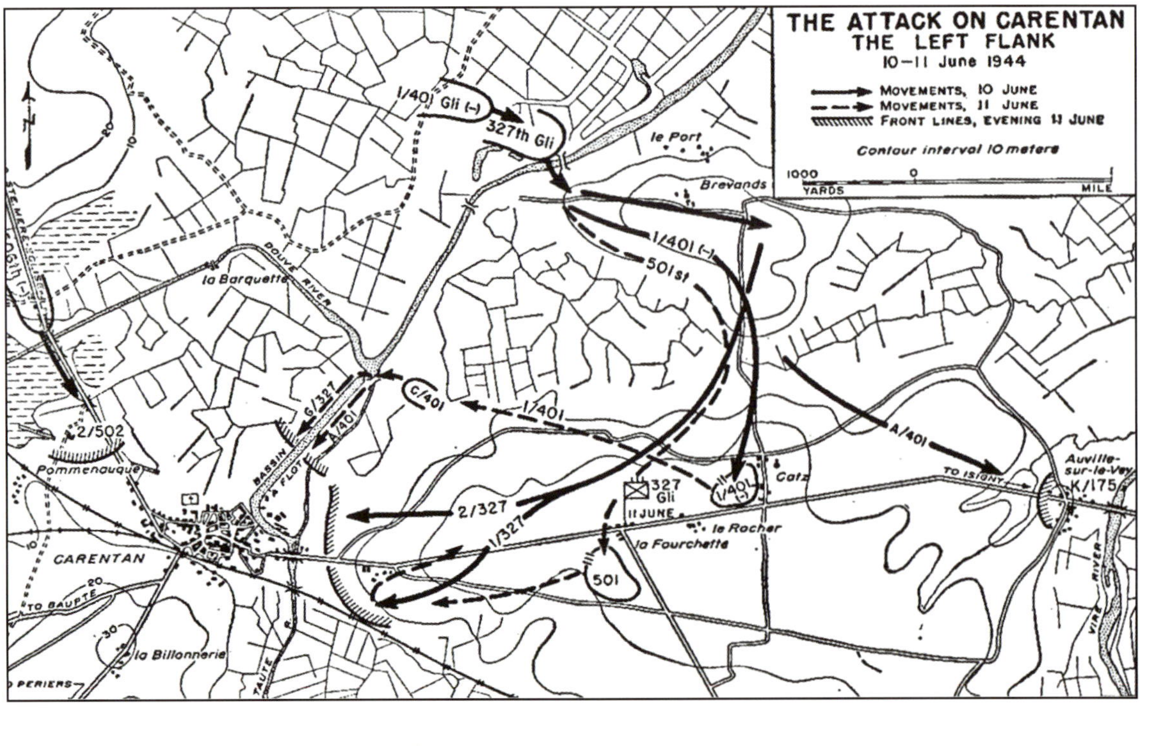

Anthony McAuliffe, 101st Airborne Artillery division commander, action on the Douve

General Anthony Clement McAuliffe (2 July 1898 - 11 August 1975) was born in Washington, D.C. He attended West Virginia University from 1916-17 and graduated from West Point in November 1918. He was a second lieutenant in 1918 and a general in 1955.

Tony McAuliffe entered the history books largely because of his famous "Nuts" remark when the 101st Airborne was encircled in Bastogne in December 1944. We tend to forget that he was also partly responsible for the capture of Carentan from 10 to 12 June 1944, and reinforcing the beachheads at Omaha and Utah Beach. He supervised the crossing of the Douve by the 327th GIR in the early hours of 10 June. He ordered a barrage to cover the crossing. Some shells fell too short and on the glidermen from C Company of the 327th, causing extensive casualties. McAuliffe would always assert that this was really the result of mines. An examination of the wounds suffered by those killed that day showed that the cause was both shell fire AND mine splinters...

McAuliffe was the artillery commander in the 101st when he parachuted into Normandy on D-Day. The Assistant Division Commander of the Division, Don Pratt was KIA on 6 June when his glider landed in Hiesville, and on 9 June, Max Taylor gave McAuliffe the responsibility of leading the decisive attack, which led to the capture of Carentan. The battle was of such great importance for the Allies that Major General Courtney Hicks Hodge, Deputy Commander of the US First Army, was in position in Brévands to supervise the battle.

For his action in Bastogne, McAuliffe was awarded the Distinguished Service Cross, pinned on to him by General Patton on 30 December 1944, later followed by the Distinguished Service Medal.

After the Battle of the Bulge, McAuliffe was given the command of his own division, the 103rd Infantry Division of the 8th American Army. He was in command of this division from 15 January 1945 to July 1945. In early May 1945, they liberated the French VIPs that were held prisoner in Itter Castle in the Austrian Tyrol.

After the War, McAuliffe occupied several military posts, including Chief Chemical Officer of the Army Chemical Corps. He returned to Europe as commander of the 7th American Army in 1953 and as Commander-in-Chief of the American Army in Europe in 1955. He was promoted to the rank of general (4-star) on 1 March 1955.

Left: Anthony McAuliffe, West Point 1918.

Below: Tony McAuliffe was the 101st artillery commander. He also acted as 101st Deputy Commander, a fictional rank, as the actual N°2 in the Division after Don Pratt's death on 6 June was really Gerry Higgins, seen here to the right during maneuvers in England. (US Army)

Right: Robert Frederick Sink, West Point, 1927. (US Army)

Robert Frederick Sink, CO 506th Parachute Infantry, pioneer and survivor...

West Point 1927. Born on 3 April 1905 in Lexington, North Carolina. Sink attended West Point in 1927. His first posting was with the 8th Infantry at Fort Screven in Georgia, with the rank of second lieutenant. In November 1929, he joined the 65th Infantry in San Juan, Puerto Rico. In March 1934, he was at Fort Meade and the 34th Infantry. He graduated from the Benning Infantry School in September 1934 and was sent to the 57th Infantry at Fort Kinley in the Philippines. In November 1937, he returned to the USA and the 25th Infantry at Fort Huachuca in Arizona from 1938 to 1940, as company commander or head of operations.

From that point, he would closely follow the development of the new US Airborne from June 1940; Commander of B Company, 501st Parachute Battalion, then S-3, and XO of the 501 PIB, then CO of the 503rd PIB. He became XO of the 503rd Parachute Infantry Regiment in March 1942 with the rank of major.

In July 1942, he was given the new 506 PIR, with the rank of Lt. Colonel in Toccoa, then Bragg. He took part in all of the Regiment's campaigns in Europe. He was the only commander of a regiment from the 101st to have been involved throughout the war. Jumpy Johnson KIA (501st), Moseley and Michaelis WIA (502nd) and George Wear (327th GIR) relieved of his command, were not so lucky. That is why the 506 is often called the Five o'Sink...

In Normandy, he was involved in an extraordinary incident worthy of a western. On 6 June, he set up the command post for his regiment in a field in Culoville between Le Holdy and Vierville. He lost contact with his 3rd battalion, which was supposed to be attacking in Brévands on the Douve. At ten in the morning, he requisitioned a Jeep from the 81st AAAB brought in by glider and its driver, T/5 George W. Rhoden. He took with him Amory Roper and Salvadore Ceniceros from his regiment and decided to go on reconnaissance around Brévands, in the company of Major Hannah, S-3 of the 506th. They joined the D-913 road in Vierville and passed a somewhat taken aback German sentry. On each side of the road, there were Germans lying around, more or less dozing. Hannah shot the sentry with his 38 caliber. The Jeep accelerated and its occupants opened fire on the Germans, who hesitated to return fire, no doubt afraid that they would hit their comrades on the other side of the road. The Jeep turned around and passed once again in front of the Germans. Its occupants killed many Germans.

In August 1945, he was Assistant Division Commander of the 101st Airborne. He was awarded the Silver Star, the Legion of Merit and the Bronze Medal. He ended his career in an administrative role at West Point, Washington and then Panama.

Sink was highly appreciated by his soldiers, who affectionately called him "Bourbon" Sink, for reasons that are easy to surmise...

Robert Frederick Sink died on 13th December 1965, and is buried in Section 1, Grave 320A at the Arlington National Cemetery.

Below: Bob Sink, 503rd Parachute Infantry Battalion CO in 1941.

Below, right: Sink at Toccoa GA with his Third Battalion CO, Bob "Bull" Wolverton, KIA at Saint-Côme-du-Mont on D-Day.

Sink appears in the middle of this famous photo, in front of the Color Guard, taken in the Place de la République in Carentan on 20 June 1944 during the medal ceremony presenting 11 Silver Stars.

1st Lt Robert Randall Harrison, I/501st Parachute Infantry, 101st Airborne, Silver Star in Carentan

In late March 1945, George S. Patton ordered Captain Abraham Baum to lead a Task Force of Combat Command B, 4th Armored Division, 50 miles behind German lines, in order to liberate the *Oflag XIII B* POW camp in Hammelburg, Germany. Officially, the reason for this highly dangerous mission was to prevent the guards from wiping out the POWs. The real reason was apparently the presence in this Oflag of Patton's son-in-law, John K Waters, who had been taken prisoner in Tunisia in 1943. The mission was a disaster. Out of the 300 men in the Task Force, 32 were killed and only 35 men made it back to American lines. The rest were taken prisoner. The 57 vehicles and tanks were destroyed. Some prisoners took advantage of the attempt to escape, but many, weakened by the lack of food, remained in the camp, which was liberated a fortnight later by the allied advance.

Among the daredevils who attempted this mission, was a hero from Carentan, 1st Lieutenant Robert Randal Harrison. A platoon leader from Item Company, 501st Parachute Infantry, involved in the attack on Hill 30 near La Billonnerie on 12 June. His company was pinned down by machine-guns and 20 mm guns on the high ground. Crawling along, Harrison managed to get to within 25 yards of a machine-gun. He gave the coordinates to the artillery who then bombarded what was practically his position. Two of his scouts were hit. He dragged them one by one to the shelter of a sunken lane, while remaining under fire. Harrison was awarded the Silver Star for his actions that day.

Harrison was taken prisoner in Wardin in Belgium on 19 December 1944. On 28 March, 1945, taking advantage of the confusion caused by Abe Baum's raid, he escaped on foot along with another officer. The two men were shot and killed as they attempted to cross a river.

Silver Star Medal, similar to the one Randall Harrison was awarded in Carentan.

3/501st helmet, with small mesh net, typical of the Holland campaign in September 1944. (Mark Bando)

The 501st circled Carentan from the east and Saint-Hilaire-Petitville on 12 June. Its Third Battalion crossed the Taute canal using the half demolished railroad bridge, and stormed Hill 30 at La Billonnerie.

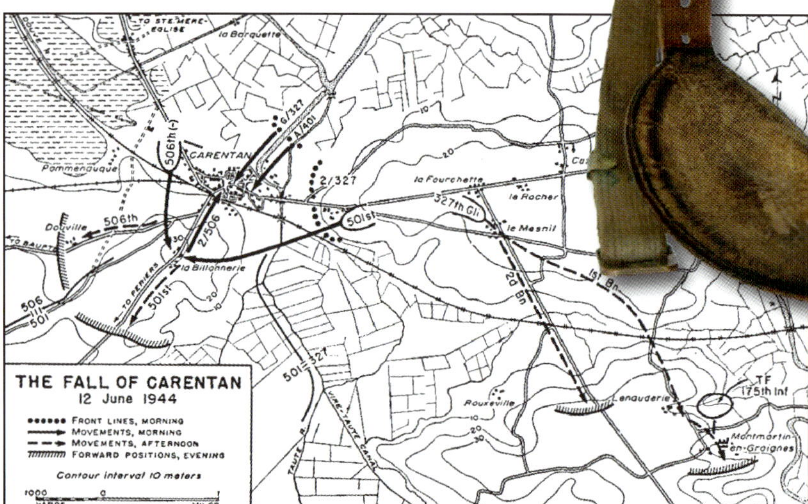

This is the half-destroyed railroad bridge used by 501st troopers to assault the heavily defended Hill 30 with its 20 mm anti aircraft guns.

Clancy Lyall, HQ 2/506th, 101st Airborne, from Carentan to Dien Bien Phu

Clarence Clancy Lyall (October 14, 1925 - March 19, 2012), a paratrooper with HQ/2/506th, then Easy Company 506th, had a Scottish father and Cherokee mother. He received one of his three war wounds in Carentan, close to a half-demolished house on rue Holgate. He was trying to get around some machine-gun posts to destroy them with a grenade when, as he entered a street, he was stabbed with a bayonet. The German was taken aback by what he had done and Clancy had time to take out his .45 and shoot him. The blade had not reached any vital organs, but Lyall was bleeding profusely. He gave himself a shot of morphine. He called a medic, and it was the famous doctor with the film star looks, Eugene Roe, from Easy 506th (Band of Brothers) who arrived, bandaged his wound and gave him a dose of morphine. He was evacuated to Utah, where he was given two more injections. During the crossing, the doctors gave him three more shots of the drug. When he got to the 92nd General Hospital in London, it was every two hours that he was given morphine. After two weeks, his wound had healed… but Clancy had become addicted to morphine. He asked to be shut up in a detox cell. He would spend four terrifying days there and would come out clean, but now wary of the drug. When he was wounded in the leg by shrapnel in early October 1944 in Opheusden (Netherlands), at the same time and alongside David K. Webster, he stubbornly refused the slightest injection, in spite of the pain…

A reminder… Clarence Odell "Clancy" Lyall signed up at Indiantown Gap in Pennsylvania in 1942 and was sent to Camp Blanding. He asked to go through Parachute School in April 1943. Having gained his jump wings, he followed courses in communications, then demolition, in August '43. From September 1943 to March 1944, he was an A stage instructor at jump school. In May '44, he joined the 2/506, and was sent to England to take part in Overlord. He jumped over Ste. Mère and landed in a tree. Wounded three times, he survived the war and when the 101st stood down in November 1945, he signed on again and found himself sent to B Company, 508 PIR. It was in this role that he took part in the Victory Parade in New York in January 1946. He decided to stay in the army, went through commando training, the Rangers and jungle fighting. In 1950, he was in the 187th PRCT and jumped in Korea at Suchon, then Munsan Ni.

Reassigned to the 101st, which was back in action in 1948, he became a special advisor. It was in this role that he was appointed advisor to the 8th French Parachute Assault Battalion and took part in Dien Bien Phu. He would be evacuated 14 days before Dien Bien Phu fell...

Lt G. William Sefton, S-2, 2/501st Parachute Infantry, 101st Airborne: It's a long way to Tipperary

G. William « Bill " Sefton, from Grand Rapids, Michigan, died on 7 December 2015. He was born in Anderson, Indiana, the son Bill Sefton, an officer who had fought in the First World War. Bill Sefton signed up at the age of nineteen. He did his training at Camp Roberts in California. He volunteered and was accepted at the Officer's Candidate School in Fort Benning.

With his second lieutenant's diploma under his belt, he volunteered for the Parachute School (TPS). With his certificate as a parachutist, he was assigned to section S-2 (Intelligence), in the second battalion of the 501st Parachute Infantry Regiment, with Robert Ballard in command. He wrote a brilliant and humorous version of his memoirs: *"It was my war and I will remember it how I like."* On D-Day, he jumped not far from the Drop Zone near Pouppeville. On 6 June, he assembled around sixty men and attacked the heights around Saint-Côme-du-Mont using bayonets. He reached Basse Addeville, then found Johnson in La Barquette. On Friday 9 June, he was recovering from his hard work near a small wall alongside a house on Dead man's corner, when a bullet hit the stone a few inches above his head. A German shooter was hiding out in the cottages in the village of Le Pont d'Ouve, on the side of the main RN13 highway. Bill grabbed his gun and guessing, shot at the window on the side of the house where the shot had come from. A GI who saw what was going on through his binoculars shouted: *"You got him, Lieutenant!"* Sefton wondered about it all his life. On 12 June, the 3/501st went on the attack at Hill 30 to the south of Carentan. Bill Sefton led his men from the S-2 platoon, 2/501st, along the RN 13 highway towards the railroad station. He crossed the Vire-Taute canal using the partially destroyed railroad track. As he made his way past houses on fire, a group of civilians came out of the cellars and thronged enthusiastically around him. An old Frenchman with a wooden leg came out with a bottle of wine singing "It's a long way to Tipperary".

Sefton would link up with Bob Sink's 506th before reaching the command post of Robert Ballard, Commanding Officer of the 2/501st, to inform him that the way to the station was clear.

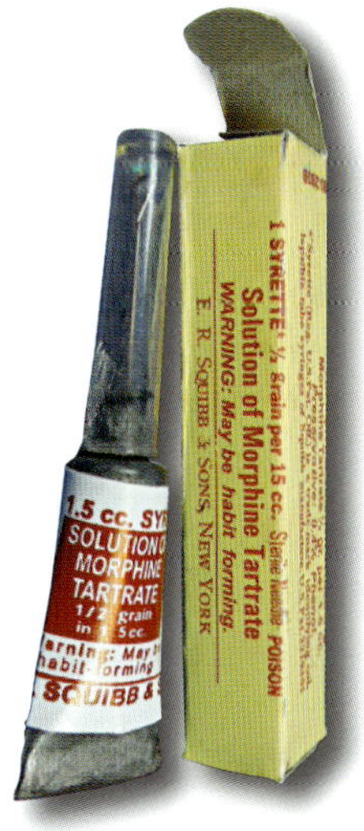

US paratroopers used this type of morphine syrette.

Left: Clacy Lyall was seriously wounded in rue Holgate, Carentan.

Right: Bill Sefton, S-2 officer, 2nd battalion 501st PIR, tasked with gathering intelligence on the enemy.

9. Halting the SS counter-attack

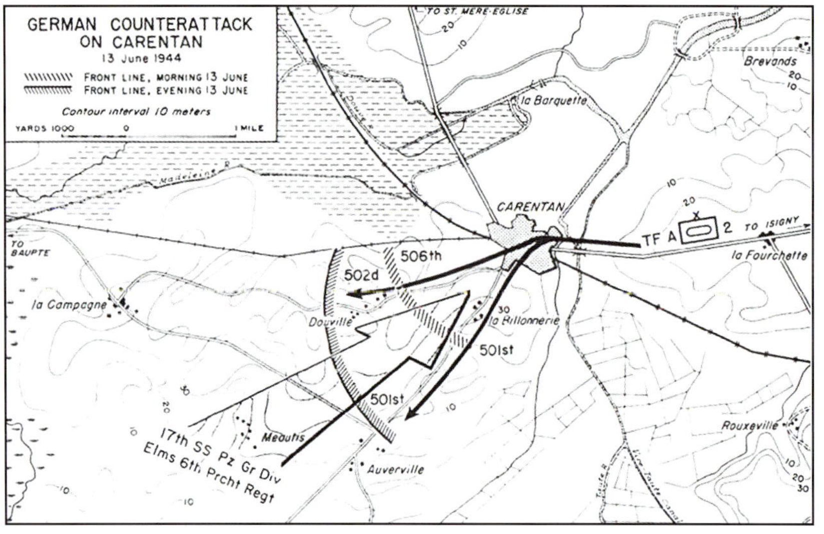

On the afternoon of 12 June, the leading elements of the *17.SS-Pz.-Gren. Div.* clashed with 501st paratroopers south of Carentan. True to their doctrine, the Germans, following an initial withdrawal, counter-attacked in strength, supported by a few self-propelled guns against the lightly-armed paratroopers; an unfavorable situation for the latter. However, tanks of the 2nd Armored Division come to the rescue and turned the tide of the battle.

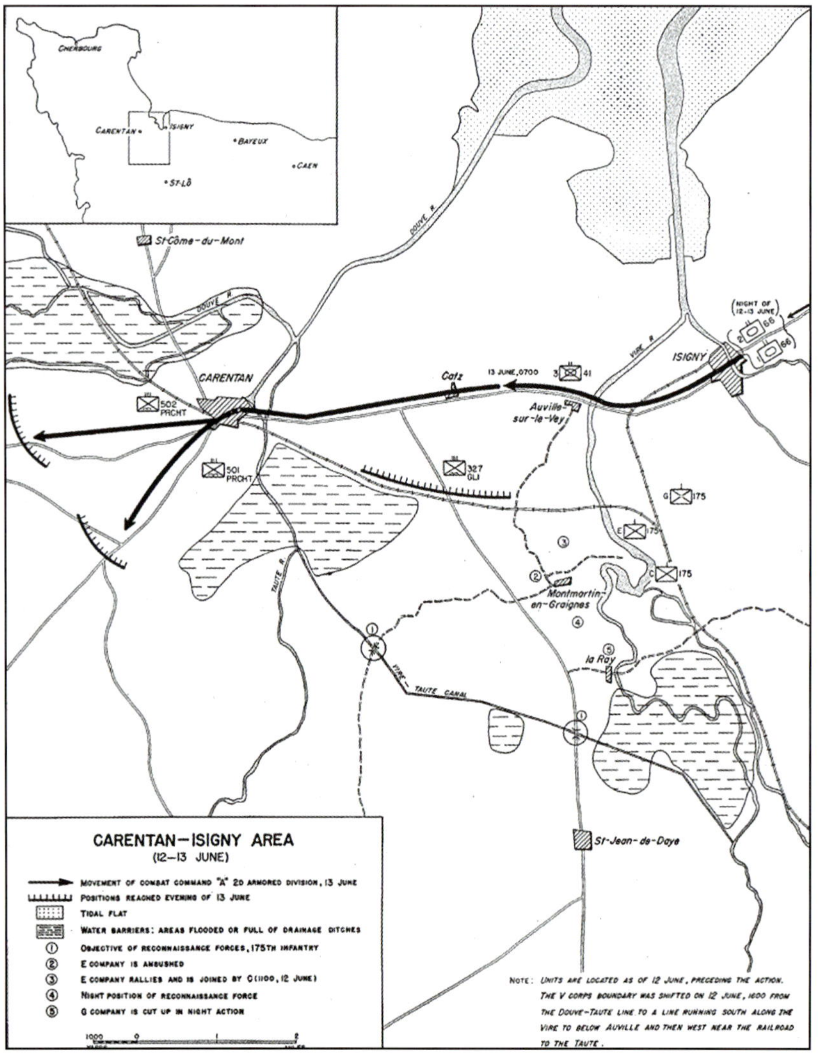

The order on the German side came directly from Hitler. Carentan had to be retaken. The 17. SS-Panzergrenadier-Division "Götz von Berlichingen" *arrived from Thouars with the mission of pushing back the Americans to the sea. Their commander,* Brigadeführer *Werner Ostendorf was furious when he learnt on 12 June that von der Heydte and his paras had pulled out of Carentan. He reassembled the SS and* Fallschirmjäger *around his armored vehicles and went on the attack at dawn on 13 June.*

The clash with the paras from the 501st and 506th PIR was horrendous. Exhausted by a week of non-stop fighting and lacking in weapons, the troopers buckled. It was the arrival of the 1st battalion of the 66th Armored Regiment of the 2nd Armored Division, that would turn things around. The 401st, attached to the 502nd was also involved. The glidermen moved in between the Shermans and made the most of the gaps in the hedges created by the tanks. While the 327th secured a line of defense alongside the railroad line to the east of Carentan, then Montmartin en Graignes, the 401st was involved in a nasty hedgerow battle in sometimes hand-to-hand fighting against the SS who stopped at nothing to prevent the tanks and paratroopers from advancing. The following account is how Captain Naugher, CO of A/401st, lost his life on 13 June. Three German officers stood in front of him waving a white flag. Eldridge Naugher came out of his shelter and it was at that point that the three German officers threw themselves to the ground, with a hidden machine-gun opening fire, ambushing and killing the A/401st commander. The Germans would be pushed back, leaving between 500 and 800 dead on the ground, according to various contradictory sources. (1) The tank crews in the 2nd Armored were given the nickname Roosevelt's butchers by their enemy.

Bloody Carentan...

Bloody Gully, Bloody Gulch... words that sound like MG 42 machine-gun fire. They sum up the confusion and violence of the fighting on 12 and 13 June 1944 to the south-west of Carentan, with three battalions from the 506th PIR up against the retreating German parachutists and the SS of the *Götz von Berlichingen* that had sped to the front from Thouars in order to push the Americans back into the sea. The clash took place to the east of

(1) See Jean-Claude Perrigault and Rolf Meister, *Götz von Berlichingen*, Editions Heimdal, 2004, p.236.

German movements south of Carentan did not go unnoticed by the American headquarters. As early as 12 June, a full Combat Command from the 2nd Armored was sent to the rescue. Under the energetic command of General Maurice Rose, the Shermans of the 66th Armored Regiment headed full-speed for Carentan.

the Carentan-Baupte railroad line alongside the D 223 road in an area of fields with high hedges and sunken lanes that the GIs called either gullies or gulches, mixing the terms up so much that 71 years later, no one really knows which part of the area they were referring to. Even the most serious historians find it hard to separate one from the other, as Mark Bando, The leading 101st Airborne specialist shows…

"*Do not confuse Bloody Gully (bloody ditch) and Bloody Gulch (bloody ravine)*"

As far as the battle for Carentan was concerned, we are talking about two different places. The writer, Ian Gardner gave his explanation in his book on the 3/506, "Tonite we die as men." Bloody Gully is to the south of the road which stretches out east to west below Donville. (D 223) Bloody Gulch is to the north of this road and on its right hand side, there is the railroad line.

The precise location of Bloody Gully remains a subject of debate. Veterans from the 3/506 did not all realize that Bloody Gully and Bloody Gulch referred to two different battles. When they talk about what happened on 12 June, the men from the 1st and 2nd battalions think they are talking about the same place as the boys in the 3/506. They talk it over together as if it was the same place, which is not really the case.

You can understand this confusion, as the pattern of fighting was the same, with each battalion from the 506th creating a front moving westwards on the same day of 12 June in a zone located to the south-west of Carentan against the same enemy, *FJ Rgt. 6* and *17. SS-Pz.Gren.-Div*. Veterans switch between the two terms, bloody gulch and bloody gully, thinking there is no difference between them.

Ian Gardner, after some long interviews with survivors from the 3/506, and with the help of diagrams, found out that the boys in the 3/506 believed their right flank was along a road, while those in the 1st and 2nd Battalions say it was the railroad track. The 101st historian, Mark Bando, continued his investigations, looking at diagrams from Lt Ronald Speirs (D/506) and Lt Dick Winters (3/506). Metal detectors revealed a number of both German and US cartridges close to the bridge under the rail track, indicating what may have been Easy Company's main line of resistance (MLR)."

On Sunday 11 June, the *FJ Regt. 6* moved out of Carentan and took up positions to the south-west of the town. They did not consider themselves as having been beaten and had just received the support of the *17. SS-Panzergrenadier-Division* "*Götz von Berlichingen*". The SS and FJ men immediately set about preparing a large-scale counter-attack with the aim of reaching St. Côme-du-Mont to push the 101st Airborne back towards the beaches.

On the following day, 12 June, HQ 101st ordered Colonel Robert Sink, CO of the 506 PIR, to set up defenses to the west of Carentan. The 1st and 2nd Battalions took up positions during the morning. At 14:00 hrs, the Germans attacked around Donville Manor and the 1/506 underwent a horrifying mortar attack around Donville. The attack was repulsed and Sink called up his 3rd Battalion, which was in reserve, to carry out a general attack by the Regiment at 05:00 hrs on the following day, 13 June. The 3rd Battalion moved in on the night of 12-13 June to join 1 and 2/506.

Joe Doughty, with the rank of Captain by war's end. As a 1st Lieutenant, he led G Company during the heavy fighting at Bloody Gulch (Ian Gardner)

G Company CO, 1st Lt Joe Doughty recalls that:

"*It was dark and damp when we took to the RN 803 (today the D 223 road to Cantepie – author's note) to look for the 1/506. That's when a motorbike came out of the fog and drew near on its way to Carentan. We stopped the biker and asked him where the 1/506 were. He got off his bike looking dumbfounded. He was a German!*"

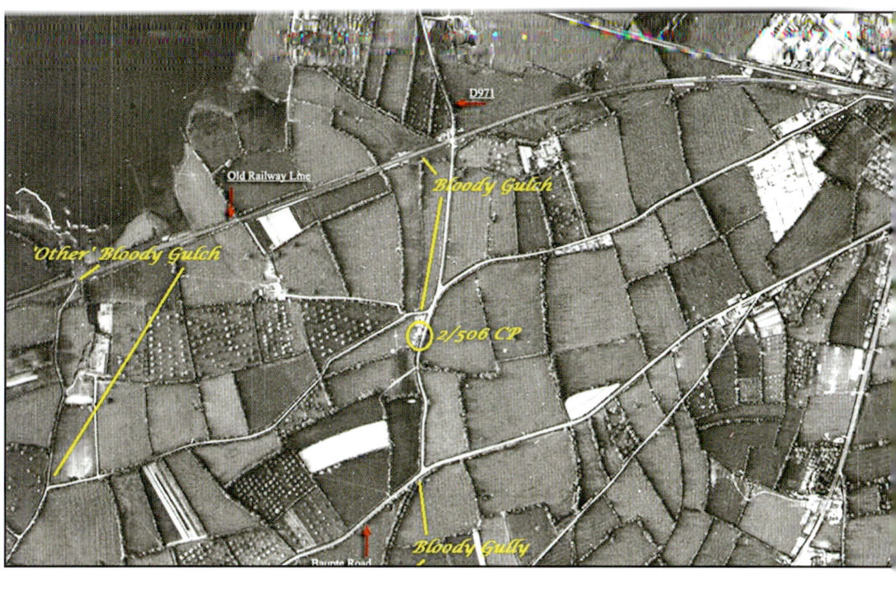

Fields in Normandy are laced with small cow paths and high hedgerows. This particular pattern created massive confusion in the memory of the veterans, between what was a gulch and what was a gully. They are located between the former Baupte railway, the Auvers road (D 223) and the D 443 to Méautis. (US Army)

The only heavy weapons available for the 101st Airborne were British 6-Pounders from the 81st Airborne Anti Aircraft Anti Tank Battalion. These guns performed well on the Auvers road, south of Carentan, against German self-propelled guns (*Sturmgeschutz*) Joe Trenge and Charles Maden operated this gun that knocked out two *Sturmgeschutz* on June 13. This Sturmegeschutz came from the Baupte road and was destroyed by Trenge with a bazooka. (Mark Bando)

60 mm mortar, Robert Houston's weapon of choice in Carentan.

Sergeant Robert Houston, H/501st Parachute Infantry, 101st Airborne, mortar star

Sergeant Robert J. Houston, using a 60mm mortar gun in H Company of the 3rd Battalion, 501st Parachute Infantry, was awarded a Distinguished Service Cross for his acts of bravery on Hill 30, at the place known as La Billonnerie to the south-east of Carentan. Houston, a gym teacher from Theresa, New York, jumped over Normandy on 6 June. He landed to the south of Carentan, along with fourteen men including his friend, Staff/Sergeant John "Mac" McMullen, a long way from his Drop Zone in Hiesville. During the first hours of the invasion, there was a game of cat and mouse between Houston, Mac and the Germans. During an exchange of fire, McMullen was wounded in the leg. The paratroopers managed to cross the Douve, probably near Le Port in Brévands, not far from the wooden bridge. Houston handed his wounded friend over to the men in the 506th. He then headed for La Barquette and made his way to Fortin farm in Pénême, where he witnessed the tragic death of Madame Odette Fortin and the young Georgette Revet, killed by a shell in the farmyard, while they were getting water from the well for the wounded men. Houston stayed with the 501st in la Barquette and only went to Vierville, the assembly area for his regiment on 9 June. Howard Johnson's 501st were given the task of going around Carentan via the east after crossing the Douve on a temporary bridge on 11 June. Houston and his battalion reached Saint-Hilaire-Petitville and crossed the Taute using the railroad bridge, half of which had collapsed.

His H Company, led by Lieutenants Curran and Herbert, was out in front and had to cross some marshland to advance towards La Billonnerie, which was well protected by mortars and 20 mm guns. Houston carried his 60 mm mortar and six shells. At the foot of the hill, the Germans opened fire with all they had at their disposal. Lieutenant Curran ordered Houston to destroy the concealed German machine-gun positions. American losses were horrendous. Lieutenant Herbert was seriously wounded in the face and Houston patched him up as best he could. American artillery used phosphorous and the shells fell short on the wounded paratroopers. Houston spotted the location of the 20 mm guns. He took up position alongside a hedge. His first shell fell a bit short. He adjusted the elevation of his barrel and launched a mortar directly into the German fortified position. He fired one shell after another and killed five men operating the 20 mm. Along with Cassada and Lenny Loyd, he rushed towards the German positions with grenades in his hand to finish off the defenders. The paratroopers showed no mercy and killed all the defenders who tried to escape. The whole of Colonel Julian Ewell's 3rd Battalion would soon reach Houston on Hill 30. Carentan was completely encircled with the 506th PIR arriving from the west. Robert Houston was injured in the ankle by shrapnel on 16 June and evacuated to Carentan, before being sent to England.

Incidentally, Houston claims to have beaten the record set by Howard Johnson in the six-mile race to the top of Mount Currahee at Camp Toccoa, Georgia.

Robert Houston, the mortar artist, won the Distinguished Service Cross for his actions in the La Billonnerie area during the 3/501st frontal assault against the Hill 30 strong point.

From Carentan to *A bridge too far*; Captain Legrand Johnson, F/502nd, 101st Airborne

This is the story of Captain Legrand King "Legs" Johnson, CO of F/502, who was awarded the Silver Star for his heroic acts in Normandy on 13 June 1944 to the south of Carentan. Robert Strayer, CO of the 2/506, seeing the massive arrival of tanks from the *17.SS* during the battle of Bloody Gulch/Gully, called the Division's CP to ask for reinforcements. Taylor sent him F/502, led by "Legs" Johnson. The young captain decided to counter attack immediately without waiting for the 2nd Armored tanks. The F/502 troopers pushed across the fields until they were encircled by the SS. Johnson was in a dire situation. Some troops stood up to surrender and were killed by the SS. Johnson then heard the characteristic noise behind him of the Sherman tanks. Leaping up and down with Lieutenant Donald Alexander (DSC, KIA 19 June), he tried to attract the attention of the US tanks, but they could not hear anything. Johnson opened fire on the American tanks and finally a commander stuck his head out and swore like a trooper. Johnson took them with him and pushed back the Germans all the way to Auvers. Legs would receive the DSC for this action, which halted the *17. SS-Pz.-Gren.-Div.* on the road to Auvers.

Legs was wounded in the shoulder on 18 September in Holland while leading his company's attack on Best. Legs refused to be evacuated by the medics until the more seriously wounded were under cover. He finally went off in a jeep, but on the way to the hospital, the vehicle came under MG 42 fire. A bullet went through his helmet, removing part of his skull. He lost consciousness and when he arrived at the hospital, the doctors overwhelmed by work, seeing his brains exposed, put him onto a pile of corpses. His sergeant, Charles Dohun went to the hospital late that afternoon to get some news about his CO. He saw Legs's body on the pile of corpses and went over to them, examining the body, which he realized was still breathing. He carried him into the operating theater and asked a surgeon to operate. The latter refused, believing it was too late. Dohun took out a Luger and threatened the doctor. The operation was a success. Legs woke up six weeks later in England, "*deaf, dumb and blind*", with a metal plate in his skull. On the contrary to what is shown in the movie, the surgeon was not accommodating and placed Dohun under arrest. Lt Col Steve Chappuis, 2/502 CO, was informed of the affair. He sent for Dohun and suspended him for one minute with his stopwatch in his hand.

F/502nd were the 101st Airborne's only reserve on 13 June 1944 when the concerted and combined attack by German paratroopers and SS Grenadiers from the *17. SS_Pz. Gren. – Div.* started. Legrand Johnson earned a Silver Star for his actions at Bloody Gulch on that day.

An American in Carentan, Edward Shames, 3/506th Parachute Infantry, 101st Airborne

Edward David Shames is one of the final major heroes of Carentan still living. Ed was promoted in just a few months from the rank of private to 2nd lieutenant during the war, receiving his promotion on the battlefield in Carentan, for his acts of bravery at the bridges near Brévands, and in the sector south of Carentan known as Bloody Gully. Born on 13 June (1922), he thought his time had come on 13 June 1944. For all these reasons, Carentan has a place of honor for him in its memory. It was also the place where he landed at around 01:40 hrs on 6 June just in front of the Gloria factory.

Edward David Shames was born in Virginia Beach, Virginia, to a Moldavian father and a Jewish mother from Belarus. Like his brothers and many other Americans, as soon as Pearl Harbor was attacked, he dreamed of signing up. Ed came across an advertisement in a national paper for a brand new service branch, the paratroops. He signed up without giving it a second thought. He was sent to Camp Lee, then Camp Toccoa in Georgia with orders to present himself to the 506th Parachute Infantry Regiment under the command of Colonel Robert Frederick Sink, or "the Fox", a West Pointer and pioneer of the new US Airborne. Ed was sent to Robert Lee Wolverton's 3rd Battalion, in Item Company, as a basic private. Wolverton soon noticed his ability to find his way, read maps and copy the topography of the area. He attached him to his team of S-3s in the Battalion. It was in this role that a few days before D-Day, Ed was given the task of making models which were as accurate as possible of the drop zones. As he was about to go off for D-Day, Ed had a nasty surprise, finding out that his place in Wolverton's plane had been given to Ward Smith, a journalist with the News of the World. This decision probably saved his life, as Wolverton and most of the passengers in this stick would be killed or captured. At 01:40 hrs on the morning of 6 June, Ed landed in front of the Gloria factory in Carentan. He made his way along the wet dock to the gates and managed to cross the Douve with four other men. After crossing the marsh, he made it to La Barquette, where he met up with Colonel Johnson, the boss of the 501st PIR, then went to Fortin farm in Pénême, which had become a field hospital and from there, and with what remained of the 3/506th, went to the bridges at Brévands. He would fight there throughout 6 and 7 June with Captain Charles Shettle, firing on the Germans on the other side of the Douve with a mortar which was missing its base plate. He could do nothing against the bombing and destruction of the bridges by the P-51 Mustangs of the 353rd US Fighter Bomber Squadron.

On the day of his 22nd birthday, Tuesday 13 June 1944, he got caught up in the confusion to the south of Carentan, facing a counter-attack from the SS in the sector of Bloody Gulch. Once again, he would stand out with his ability to analyze battle strategy and his bravery under fire as he communicated with the command posts. For all of his acts during this first week of the invasion in Carentan, he was promoted to 2nd lieutenant and awarded a Distinguished Service Cross.

Right: Ed Shames, 22 years old, on Tuesday, 13 June.

Below: the Gloria milk factory in Carentan, where Ed Shames landed on 6 June, before moving out along the wet dock and swimming across the river. This milk plant had been bought before the war by an American company, the Carnation Milk Company. Imagine the troopers surprise when, as Harold Stedman of F/502nd did, picked up cans bearing the name of a company they had worked for stateside. (US Army)

2nd Armored; Roosevelt's butchers! (Private collection)

Men of the 41st Armored Infantry Regiment of the 2nd Armored Division wore camouflaged HBT two-piece or overalls during the early days of the Invasion. (Michel Quilez collection)

M7 Priest of the 2nd Armored crossing the railroad in rue Holgate, Carentan. (US Army)

General Maurice Rose and Roosevelt's butchers. The 2nd Armored Division's tanks were decisive in the liberation of Carentan

The son and grandson of rabbis, Maurice Rose signed up at the age of 15 as a soldier in General Pershing's army to go and fight in Mexico before the First World War. He was thrown out when it was discovered he was too young.

Rose kept trying and, at the age of 17, obtained a diploma at the First Officers training camp in Fort Riley, Kansas, receiving his appointment as 2nd lieutenant. He set off with the US Expeditionary Forces for France and was wounded at Saint Mihiel. Between the wars, he would leave the army, initially to become a travel agent, but he was soon back again, obtaining the rank of captain specializing in armored vehicles.

During the Second World War, he was part of the 1st Armored Division in Africa. He was the first officer to accept the surrender of a large Nazi unit.

After that, he was appointed chief of Staff of the 2nd Armored Division. He was awarded his first Silver Star in Sicily in 1943. On 7 June 1944, he went ashore in Normandy with the 2nd Armored. He was asked on 12 June to support the 101st Airborne in Carentan with his Combat Command A, including in particular, the 66th Armored Regiment, the 82nd Armored Reconnaissance Bn, 2 Bns from the 41st Armored Infantry Regiment, the 14th AFA Bn and the 92d AFA Bn.

On Tuesday 13 June, Rose sent his reconnaissance units out. At 03:22 hrs, he gathered his forces in Les Vers near Isigny. At 04:00 hrs, the Reconnaissance Co from the 66th AR came under attack from several panzers and by the infantry. The D/66 was detached and sent to Carentan to assist the 101st on mopping up the western side of the town but, before the operation could begin, the unit was recalled to repulse with the 2/66, the German counter-attack on Carentan.

Armored vehicles from the 2nd Armored and 101st paratroopers would repulse the armor of the *17. SS-Pz.-Gren.-Div. "Götz von Berlichingen* throughout the day with such efficiency that the Germans would call the 2nd Armored, Roosevelt's Butchers.

In August 1944, Rose was given command of the 3rd Armored Division. Although he was a general, he was always up at the front. Under his command, his unit would manage to cover 106 miles in just one day. The 3rd Armored played a huge role in several campaigns and was the first to cross the Siegfried line.

On 30th March 1945, in the Paderborn region in Germany, General Rose was with a task force. He was in one of the three Jeeps, along with two motor bikes and under the cover of an armored car. The group was moving along a muddy road in the woods when it was split in two by shots from automatic weapons. One of the tanks in the task force was destroyed, along with one of the Jeeps accompanying the General. His own Jeep ended up in a ditch. Seeing the enemy tanks arriving, he ordered to push ahead. The enemy fired flares. Rose's Jeep came face to face with a German armored vehicle that had come out of the woods, then a second one and then a third. The commander of the German tank ordered the Americans to surrender. Maybe he saw General Rose going for his weapon? He opened fire with his machine-gun killing the General instantly.

The driver of the command Jeep (T/5 Shaunce) and Major Bellinger managed to escape and hide in the woods.

On that day, the US Army lost one of its greatest soldiers and perhaps the most highly specialized commander. A hero in Carentan, General Maurice Rose is buried in the American cemetery in Margraten (Netherlands).

Right: A true American hero, General Maurice Rose.

Below: March 1945, Maurice Rose is awarded the French Croix de Guerre by General Louis Koeltz.

Joe Pangerl, an original "Ritchie Boy" in Carentan... Here on the left with his IPW team of the 502nd.

Joseph Pangerl; German speakers for the interrogation of German prisoners of war

Captain Joe Pangerl was in charge of interrogation section N°1 (IPW N°1 =Interrogators of Prisoners of war) of the 502nd Parachute Infantry Regiment. His role was to obtain information from prisoners of war. Originally from Austria, Pangerl emigrated at the age of three, but was a fluent speaker of German. He was an original Ritchie Boy. Ritchie Boys were soldiers who were mainly of German and Austrian Jewish origin that the US Army brought together because of their special ability to obtain information. They were trained at Camp Ritchie in Maryland before being sent to various units, which explains their nickname.

The Ritchie Boys were a group of around 10,000 young mainly Jewish Germans who, having had fled Nazi Germany, enlisted in the US Army. They did their training at the Military Intelligence Training Center, also known as Camp Ritchie, in Maryland, where they were given special training in modern psychological warfare. Because of their knowledge of the language, culture and German mindset, they were much better than American soldiers in taking up this role, the main goal of which was to study the enemy and wear him down to obtain his unconditional surrender.

On 5 July 1944, Pangerl was at a farm near Cherbourg in the company of two other linguists attached to the Regiment, 1st Lt. Nicholas Ermolieff and Lieutenant Robert Judels, both of Russian origin, who were tasked with interrogating prisoners from the East, the famous volunteers from the Ukraine, Georgia, Mongolia, who were more or less forced to enroll in the German Army. All of these men belonging to the Intelligence section of the 502nd PIR were examining weapons taken from the Germans. Suddenly, the weapon that Judels was holding fired and Ermolieff was killed instantly.

It should be said that each parachute regiment in the 101st Airborne, 506th, 502nd and 501st, was organized in their own way as far as their intelligence section, S-2, was concerned. In the 501st, it was just a small group of men the size of a platoon (35 men), divided into a small reconnaissance section, which was sent behind enemy lines, often to take prisoners. In the 502nd and 506th, the section was even smaller, but the men rarely carried out such expeditions behind German lines. They stayed further back studying the reports taken from the enemy. During the war, these sections were under the command of Benjamin Wax (501st), George Buker (502nd) and William Leach (506th). Each command company (HQ) also had around six men in an S-2 section, including one soldier who spoke fluent German. These six men under the command of a lieutenant carried out many patrols behind enemy lines.

Joe died on 24th November 2013. He was awarded the French Legion of Honor in 2011.

Joe Pangerl with his A2 leather jacket and the "widow-maker" regimental patch.

10. GRAIGNES

Above: Graignes, a peaceful little village on the edge of the marshes south of Carentan. It would find itself in the path of history and the theater of tough fighting.

Below: the Rigault family symbolizes the Graignes population's engagement alongside the paratroopers. They are seen here in July 1944, following fighting opposite their farm. The father, Gustave, and his children, Marthe, Odette and Jean-Claude used this punt to recover a large quantity of American equipment that had been dropped in the marshes. They then helped evacuate survivors of the battle, hiding twenty-one Americans in their barn.

The small commune of Graignes in the heart of the marshes in the Cotentin peninsula entered the history books from the first days of the Battle of Normandy. Its name is associated with two historic events. Unfortunately, rather like Oradour-sur-Glane, it is known for the atrocious acts and fires caused by the SS troops. But it is also known for the heroic American deeds carried out there in an incident reminiscent of El Alamo, when 182 paratroopers would hold out until to the last round in the fortified village, with the help of French civilians to at least slow down, if not stop, the arrival of an SS armored division at a crucial moment of the fighting. The goal of the Germans was to push the Americans back to the sea and prevent the formation of a real beachhead from Omaha and Utah Beach. The martyred village made the decision to leave its fate in the hands of these lost paratroopers during a bloody battle which, in the end, stalled the advance of the 17.SS enough to allow the American armored vehicles that had come ashore on Omaha Beach, to join the exhausted 101st Airborne troopers and, on 13 June, carry out the liberation of Carentan, thus blocking the link-up points of the American beachheads...

Captain Abraham Sophian, surgeon with the 3/507th Parachute Infantry, 82nd Airborne, and martyr of Graignes

Captain Abraham 'Bud' Sophian Jr was born on 27 April 1915 in Kansas City, the son of a respected Jewish doctor. Bud was a man of great intelligence, a "Renaissance Man". His academic background was faultless. At the age of 14, he joined the Phillips Academy in Andover, Massachusetts, a preparatory school for the elite. Then, he went to Stanford University in Los Angeles, one of the most famous schools on the West Coast. He started to study medicine there but moved to Cornell, near New York, which was also one of the best schools in the country. Bud excelled at golf and swimming, was a quarterback in the football team and wrestled... He did his hospital training at Mount Sinai Hospital in Cleveland, and graduated in 1941, getting married fifteen days later. On 17 August 1942, Bud entered the army as a first lieutenant in the 31st Medical Regiment at Camp Berkeley in Texas. He grew extremely bored there and wanted to do something more useful. He volunteered for the paratroops, and found himself at the Parachute School in Fort Benning, with the 507th PIR in June 1943. He was sent to the 3rd Battalion of the 507th PIR as a surgeon with the rank of captain. He jumped on 6 June 1944 from plane N° 47, tail number 42-92773, with Serial N° 25 out of the 72 in the 53rd Troop Carrier Squadron, which transported the 507th RHQ. His stick comprised of 16 men. He was the second to jump after Captain Richard Chapman. Pfc Franck P. Costa was the ninth in his stick. He found himself on the ground near Graignes to the south of Carentan. Rapidly the American force included 170 men from the 3rd/507th and a dozen boys from the 501st PIR, totaling in all 170 soldiers and 12 officers (some say 14), then a glider pilot, two French policemen and 14 Basque prisoners as well as two soldiers from the 29th Infantry Division. The officers were, among others, Major Charles D. Johnson, Captain Leroy D. Brummitt, S-3 with the 3rd/507th, Captain Richard Chapman, First Lieutenants, Elmer F . Hoffman and Earle R. Reed, Francis E. Naughton, Lowell C. Maxwell, Elmer Farnham, Willard E. Chambers, H. Edward Wagner, 2nd Lt William A. Comstock, George C. Murn (501st)... On the evening of 11 June, after repelling many attacks from superior and better-armed SS forces (2nd bn. of *SS-Panzergrenadier-Regiment 38*, of the *17. SS-Panzergrenadier-Division "Götz von Berlichingen"*) (1), the surviving troopers fired a distress flare from the church tower in Graignes. This was the signal. Captain Brummitt gave the order to all his troopers who were able to walk to set out across the marshes. In small groups, with between two and twenty men, the paratroopers, who were running short of munitions, tried to escape by heading for Carentan. Brummitt and Naughton assembled 60 troopers or so around them. At noon on 12 June, some French civilians led the way across the marshland. On the evening of 13 June, they met up with a patrol from the 2nd Armored near Carentan. On the morning of Monday 12 June, SS soldiers in black uniforms entered Graignes from every side. Captain Bud Sophian was in the church. Three GIs were lying there, seriously wounded during the fighting. 14 others suffered from lighter wounds. Sophian came out of the Church waving a white flag. He hoped that the Germans would respect the Geneva Convention. What happened next is still vague and there are contradictory stories. We can however suppose that the three seriously wounded men were finished off in the Church by the SS. Five other seriously wounded men, who were able to stand up, were pushed outside of the church towards a small pond in front of Madam Boursier's café. They were savagely killed by bayonet. Some left for dead would suffer in pain for a long time before dying. Father Leblastier and the Franciscan monk, Charles Lebarbanchon, were murdered at the same time as their helpers, Eugénie Dujardin and Madeleine Pezeril. According to witnesses, nine GIs were spotted in a field near Le Mesnil Angot digging their own grave. They were all shot in the head. The months that followed were very confused. Because of the fighting, the civilians were evacuated. When the witnesses returned, US Grave Registration personnel had recovered the bodies and buried them in temporary cemeteries, including the one at Blosville. However, Bud Sophian's body was not among the nine exhumed at Mesnil-Angot. It would appear that he was separated from the troopers and taken a little further away where he was shot, probably along with Captain Loyal Bogart, CO of B/501st. Bogart had been hit by flak just before jumping. He could have returned to England, but he preferred to jump and that is how he found himself in the hell of Graignes. Sophian's body was buried by a farmer half a mile or so from Graignes on the road to Tribehou.

A Jewish doctor, Abraham Sophian could have remained safely behind in the United-States. Instead, he volunteered for service with the paratroops and chose to confront the SS troops at Graignes after his comrades had withdrawn, in order to protect wounded men who were unable to move. He would pay for this with his life, summarily executed near Tribehou along with two other officers, Loyal Bogart and Charles Johnson.

(1) Only the *II Bataillon* of *SS-Panzergrenadier-Regiment 38 (II./38)* was at that time signaled as being in this sector. On 10 June: "*Weak elements of II./38 (SS-Hstuf. Rethmeyer) had advanced beyond the Vire-Taute canal, towards Isigny-sur-Mer, as far as Montmartin-en-Graignes. The 8.(schwere)/38 (heavy company) reached its observation post on Hill 35 without coming under attack. In this region, the motorized detachments of Regiment 38 were then brought up.*" According to the Division's history that was published by Heimdal in 2004, written by Jean-Claude-Perrigault, page 232. No fighting was signaled by the Germans in the Graignes sector. The bulk of the fighting was carried out against Carentan and only a few German soldiers must have been in the Graignes sector. It is still a mystery today. (publisher's note)

Captain Loyal Bogart, B/501st, leader to the end

The number of men 501st men present in Graignes is still open to debate; was it 18, 20? They belonged to B Company and HQ Company in the 1/501st. The Commanding Officer of B/501st was among them. Captain Loyal K. Bogart was hit by flak in his C-47 on the night of 6 June. He insisted on jumping with his men and broke his leg on landing. He managed to reach Graignes, in the middle of the marshes. Although injured, he nevertheless wanted to do something useful. Placed in the school in Graignes, which had become the command post for the 182 paratroopers gathered in Graignes under command of Major Johnson of the 507th PIR, 82nd Airborne, he would be the phone operator for the various outposts around the village. The school was heavily bombarded by the Germans on 10 June to the extent that the ceiling fell in on Bogart and on Major Johnson of the 507th.

When the Germans, probably the advance troops of *II.SS-Panzergrenadier-Regiment 38*, *17. SS "Götz von Berlichingen"*, entered the village, they murdered four civilians and 24 wounded troopers, including men from the 501st, Private William H Love, HQ/1/501 PIR, Roy M Callahan, T/4 Co B 501 PIR.

Bogart who was still alive, was dragged out of the ruins. He was taken along with the 3/507th surgeon, Bud Sophian and Johnson to the Tribehou road. After interrogating them, the Germans ordered them to kneel down and shot them in the neck. Their bodies, covered by the undergrowth, were only found in 1945. Also among the victims were Herb Weiss, Jimmie Millican and Raymond Hoffman, all from HQ/1 501 PIR.

Opposite: Captain Loyal Bogart, shot at Tribehou, along with at least thirteen of his comrades, including Herb Weiss (**Right**) from his B Company, 501st PIR...

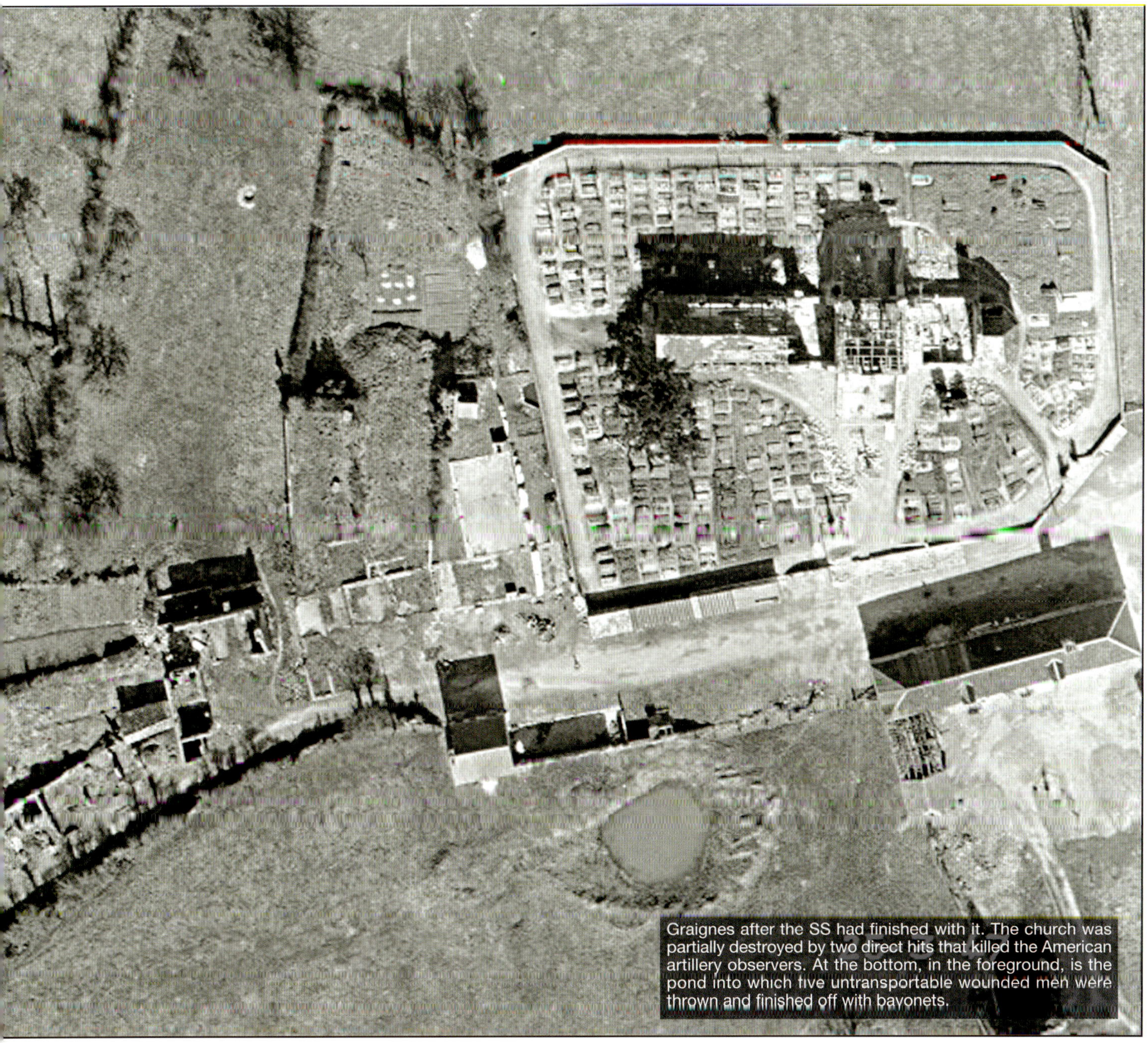

Graignes after the SS had finished with it. The church was partially destroyed by two direct hits that killed the American artillery observers. At the bottom, in the foreground, is the pond into which five untransportable wounded men were thrown and finished off with bayonets.

Another view of Graignes with, on the right, the Boursier café, turned into a mess for the soldiers thanks to the generosity and hard work of Madame Boursier and Mayor Voydie. On the left is the school house which was used as a headquarters by the Americans.

EPILOGUE, LEST WE FORGET...

Above: Carentan is damaged but free. The town would suffer from heavy American shelling throughout the night of 10 to 11 June, then by German artillery which lasted for several weeks after its liberation.

Right: These are Glidermen of the 327th Glider Infantry Regiment, recognizable from their helmet markings. They were the first to enter the town in the early hours of 12 June 1944. They are seen here in Place Vauban.

André Boucherie, in black, talking with GIs after the town was liberated…

"Welcome to Carentan"
Major John Maginnis, Civil affairs and Military Government USA

Major John J. Maginnis was an officer in the Civil Affairs and Military Government of the USA during the Second World War. The CA/MG's mission was to control and ensure the safety of the civilian populations in war and occupied zones. On 1 April 1944, Maginnis was named Commander of C Detachment (C2B1), with five officers and nine soldiers appointed to VII Corps, 1st US Army. He would be the first officer of a detachment from Civil Affairs to set foot in France with the 101st Airborne Division. On 8 June 1944, he came ashore in a DUKW on Utah Beach and headed for the 101st command HQ in Hiesville, where he reported to Colonel Ned Moore, the Division's G-1. It was only on 11 June that his detachment was allowed to advance towards Saint-Côme-du-Mont, where Maginnis helped in the fighting along the road to Carentan to liberate the town. On the following day, Monday 12 June, Maginnis entered the town aboard his Jeep. Here is an extract from his war journal:

"Entered Carentan at 11:00 hrs leading my detachment from Civil Affairs. Set up in the Town Hall. Contacted the Mayor, Monsieur Joret, the chief of police, Fire chief and the town's officials. Took measures concerning fires, street cleaning and restoring the movement of traffic. A lot of progress was made. The Mayor, Doctor Caillard was dead. No electricity. No running water. Only the pumps still worked."

"The place was a mess. Houses were on fire. There were German soldiers lying dead in the streets in amongst piles of destroyed equipment. The roads were blocked with walls falling down or with large gaping holes. We could hear close by in the south, shots from light arms. I went straight to the Town Hall, which was partly destroyed, and totally deserted. I decided to gather together all the town officials. The deputy mayor, the chiefs of police and fire, as well as a doctor turned up. I learnt that the Mayor, Monsieur Jean Baptiste Caillard, had been killed by a bomb from one of our planes on 10th June. It was his deputy, Monsieur Albert Joret who was replacing him. He was already quite elderly. He was so crippled that he used a cane to walk. He was dressed all in black. His shoulders were rounded and he had a white beard. In French, he asked me if I spoke French and I replied in the affirmative. 'Thank God for that," he replied, "I'm so happy and relieved, as I don't speak a word of English." Holding out his hand, he said simply and without the slightest irony, as he would to any other visitor, "Welcome to Carentan." The man had spent his whole life in this quiet backwater of France, and now found himself with some huge responsibilities because of the torment of the war. After spending six days holed up in his cellar, he came out to find his town had been destroyed and full of strange soldiers with whom he could not communicate. This was the start of a warm relationship that I will always cherish. Monsieur Joret told me he would do everything he could to help me and asked his assistants to do everything I asked of them."

John Maginnis was a US Army Civil Affairs officer who became a friend to Carentan. He would make a significant contribution to getting the town back on its feet after its liberation. He is seen here in September 1944.

This photo is charged with symbolism for the reconstruction of Carentan. The men tasked with the reconstruction are seen here in what is today's wedding ceremony room at the Carentan town hall: Captain J. A. Herman, British Army, Dr. Léon Simon, Major John Maginnis, US Army, and the Mayor of Carentan, Albert Joret, who had taken over from *Docteur* Caillard who had been killed in the bombardments of 6 June.

Maginnis would have to hastily leave Carentan during the German counter-attack on 13 June, when they reached the area around the railroad station. He returned on 14 June and began work on the reconstruction and reorganization of the town. In the eighties, he gave the Don Pratt Museum at Fort Campbell the key to Carentan Town Hall that he had kept as a souvenir…

John J. Maginnis served during the First and Second World War, then as a Reserve Officer. He was a lieutenant in the 301st Infantry Regiment of the 76th Infantry Division in the American Expeditionary Force during the First World War in France. He then served in Europe in 1944 with the rank of major, then lieutenant colonel, and colonel, in Normandy and then in Belgium in a detachment from Civil Affairs. The Civil Affairs division was in charge of security and the well-being of the civilian population in war and occupied zones and maintained law and order. They also had to ensure that civilians did not interfere with ongoing military operations. Once this mission was complete, Civil Affairs was expected to hand over authority and power to the civilian body in the country concerned.

Military Government Journal – John Maginnis

General Troy Middleton, VIII US Corps commander, of which the 101st Airborne was part of in Normandy, awards the Silver Star to Bruno Schroeder (HQ/506th) during the 20 June 1944 ceremony in the Place de la République, watched by the mayor, Albert Joret.

From 20 June onwards, sporadic but regular German shellfire on the town forced the 101st Airborne Division headquarters to set up along the wet dock.

Chaplain Tilden McGee, of the 3rd Battalion, 506th, holds a service in the Place de la République after the fighting. He would become a POW in Holland.

Nicholas J. Neises (F/502nd), or the tragic end for a prisoner of war in Normandy

The episode is not very well known, but remains a vivid memory for those involved. It involves the suffering of the paratroopers taken prisoner in Normandy and brutally forced to march to the rear, all the while subjected to the unending machine-gun fire from planes that were, nevertheless, those of the Allies. 5th Grade Technician, Nicholas J. Neises (F/502nd) was taken prisoner in the first hours of D-Day near Ecausseville, a long way from his drop zone. He was only just 24. Like dozens of other troopers, he would discover the horrifying conditions suffered by the POWs in Normandy. He was first taken towards Cherbourg, then towards Bricquebec. The walk was exhausting and they were not given water or food. They had to walk barefoot on the stony paths, as the Germans had taken their boots. Transfer by truck was horrible, as in the skies P 47s reigned over Normandy and relentless attacked every vehicle. The German guards jumped into the ditches to shelter, but forced the POWs to remain in the trucks. On 11 June, Nicholas "Bud" Neises was walking towards Besneville along with 23 other prisoners. Suddenly, two low-flying Polish Spitfires appeared and opened fire on the column of prisoners. Nicholas was killed instantly. He would not go through the terrifying experience of Starvation Hill at the military equestrian center in Saint Lô or the Troisgots Seminary, where the Germans gathered and starved the prisoners from the Battle of Normandy, including a large number of 101st and 82nd Airborne paratroopers (1). Nicholas Neises was married with a young son. His family would only learn of his death in August 1944. Incidentally, Nicholas had been on detachment as Winston Churchill's bodyguard when the Prime Minister visited the 101st Airborne in Welford on 23rd March 1944.

(1) We should be reminded that survival conditions for German POWs in American and French camps were terrible. In the sole camp of Ebensee in Austria, 12,000 men die, many in captivity or during battlefield clearance duties. (publisher's note)

Nicholas J. Neises, "Bud", F/502nd, killed on 11 June by allied aircraft at Besneville, along with twenty-two other American prisoners.

André Ledran, a Carentan civilian in the battle

It's a little-known fact, but Carentan and its surroundings experienced the horrors of war as early as June 1940, with bombardments, naval artillery fire and the exodus of refugees. Painful episodes that would occur once more, and with more intensity, four years later. André Ledran's childhood years were at the heart of these two episodes. This is what he said: *"I was born in Carentan in 1933 and lived there up to 1949, the date on which I went to off to teacher training school in Trouville. My mother, father and their eight children, lived at 23 rue Giesmard, the road coming from Saint Hilaire bridge, just before the gendarmes' station. The arrival of the Germans in 1940 was a difficult period for us. To us, and especially my father, who had fought in the Great War, it was unthinkable that the Germans could get as far as Normandy. The German thrust was preceded by the arrival of numerous refugees, many of whom were Belgian and Dutch, escaping the fighting. We feared the 'Fifth Column", German saboteurs dressed as civilians and the Gendarmes arrested many Dutch men for questioning. We also feared parachutists. Older men, like my father, kept their hunting rifles at their side, ready to hunt down any parachutists. There were also a lot of British soldiers moving up towards Cherbourg in order to sail back home. There were a lot of military convoys jamming the main RN13 road, which passed in front of our home.*

This photo shows American troops going down rue Holgate towards the railroad crossing overlooked by the "Désiré Ingouf" house, towards the south and the German counter-attack. (US NARA)

81st Airborne Anti-Aircraft Bn. 6-Pounder gun in rue Holgate, Carentan. (US Army)

Destruction can been seen in rue Holgate as 101st Airborne troopers march down it to encounter the German counter-attack of 13 June. (US Army)

Above: the intersection of the Auvers and Périers road, the approach route of the 2nd Battalion, 506th PIR during the capture of Carentan on 12 June. (US Army)

Below: a short rest for these troops in rue Holgate before marching south to take on the *Waffen-SS* of the *Götz von Berlichingen*... (US Army)

My father worked as a maintenance man at the Gloria factory in Carentan. He had been asked, in June 1940, to make concrete obstacles to halt the German tanks. The desire to stop the Germans was very strong, especially for my father who had been victorious in the Great War. This generation of Great War soldiers was, in 1940, greatly dismayed, unable to understand how "The War to end all wars" had led us, twenty years later, to this disaster.

The French fight along the Douve river

The French, led by sailors, put up a great fight at the bridges over the Douve (1). *The bridge over the Douve was blown and there were artillery guns at Saint Côme. Le Courbet, an old battleship from the previous war, was in the Beys bay. It fired on the roads leading to Carentan in order to slow down Rommel's troops. Léon Gauthier, who would go on to be one of the 177 Kieffer commandos, was an apprentice gunner on Le Courbet which was firing on Carentan. A schoolfriend was killed by the blast from a naval shell. The fighting ceased at around three in the afternoon on 18 June 1940. The defensive line was drawn up along the ways to Prétot, Carentan and La Haye du Puits. The Germans were halted there, along the RN 13 road, and they suffered losses. Our temporary schoolhouse was opposite the Javel factory and*

All the available forces of the exhausted 101st Airborne converged towards Donville and Méautis. The liberated town of Carentan was threatened by the German counter-attack. Men make their way down rue Holgate towards the front line. A medical unit is seen here followed by a captured German vehicle. (US Army)

was riddled with impacts that bore witness to the fighting of 1940.

My father decided to leave when the Germans arrived. We went to stay with a cousin at Méautis, accompanied by several other families. Men aged between 20 and 40 had been called up and it was only men older than 40 who remained, those who had been through 1914-1918. They hated the Germans but they knew how to reassure the population. It was them who, in 1944, made shelters and trenches for the civilians. In my road there were many widows or women whose men were away and it was the older men who reassured them. So we left along the road known as the "six ways" by the road leading from Auvers to Méautis. At the "six ways", there was a crossroads where we rested for a while, near the Sénoville farm. At the crossroads was a German artillery unit that was firing on ponts d'Ouve. There was a tall German officer bellowing orders from his command vehicle.

Troopers of the 501st PIR, probably from the 3rd Battalion, link-up with the 506th PIR. (US Army)

(1) The 1940 fighting: An armored column of Rommel's *7. Pz.-Div.* arrived in the Carentan area on 18 June and was tasked with capturing the port of Cherbourg. The old battleship, Courbet, sailed into the baie des Veys at 5 am and fired on the column with its twelve 305 mm guns, firing a total of 112 shells. The column was unable to continue north and had to change direction, crossing the Cotentin from east to west then heading up towards Cherbourg along the western side of the peninsula.

The 112 shells fired by *Le Courbet* on 18 June were done so between 13:00 and 19:30 hrs;

- the first, with 38 shells, between 13:00 and 14:05 hrs fell on the Isigny-Carentan road, at the "la Fourchette" crossroads.

- The second, with 33 shells, at around 15:00 hrs, fell on a crossroads situated south of Carentan.

- The next salvo, with 41 shells, was at 17:00 hrs on the same target. It should be noted that the Courbet was not the only ship to open fire on 18 June.

It should be noted that Le Courbet was not the only ship to open fire on 18 June.

- *Le Léopard* and *Le Savorgnan de Brazza*, sailing off the west coast of the Cotentin fired respectively forty-four 130 mm shells and ninety 138 mm shells on the Flamanville-Les Pieux road, between 12:10 and 12:35 hrs.

- The same ships fired respectively fifty-six 130 mm shells and sixty-six 138 mm shells on Portbail between 18:57 and 19:39 hrs.

At around midnight on 18 June, the bridge at Pont-L'Abbé was blown. At 01:30, the Pont des Veys collapsed into the Vire. At 02:30, it was the Pont Douve's turn to be destroyed.

At Pont-Douve, below the hill of Saint-Côme-du-Mont, the day of 18 June was hectic but victorious; the soldiers of the *208e Régiment d'Infanterie* had held the Germans with the help of the *Courbet* battleship, escorted by the destroyers, *Flore* and *Melpomène*.

The position at Saint-Côme-du-Mont, commanded by *lieutenant de vaisseau* Bureau, comprised, on 18 June:

- at Saint-Côme, a group led by *capitaine* Langlois.

- at the Rampau farm, with 80 sailors, commanded by *enseigne de vaisseau* Blampain. These men had only one 75 mm gun and the expected other three failed to turn up at the position.

- At the bridge over the Douve, there were three 75 mm guns, under the orders of *Enseigne de Vaisseau* Bastard, two 13.2 mm machine-guns, two 25 AC guns, two 8 mm machine-guns and two light machine-guns. There was also a British infantry company with two anti-tank guns and two LMG, led by Major Moody.

- At the La Barquette lock there were two 8 mm machine-guns and two LMG.

At 07:30 on 18 June, three German vehicles were destroyed in front of this position.

As was the case with all of the lines around Carentan, the French sailors were ordered to lay down their weapons at 16:15 hrs on 19 June, following the fall of Cherbourg.

The resistance put up at the Douve bridges would notably permit 30,630 men of the British 2nd Infantry Division and the "Norman Force" to board ship at Cherbourg and reach England.

The 101st Airborne paratroopers arrive where other heroes of Carentan, the firefighters, are busy trying to put out a fire, getting teenagers to help to pump water for the fire hose.

I have always remembered this scene because I could see my father, filled with hate for the "Boche". He did not say a thing because he had to protect our group. We moved into a hay barn at my cousin's at Méautis. We stayed there for two days, until the situation calmed down a bit.

A year of deprivation

Life carried on under the occupation and with its deprivations. The first year was really hard as we were not prepared for it. I ate at a canteen that was run by a charitable organization, but there was not much to eat there. The canteen was set up near the cemetery, in a very dusty former broom-making workshop. After this first year, the population became more organized in finding food.

My father knew all about agriculture. We had a small yard behind the house and the Gloria factory, as well as the town hall, opened workers' allotments. Thanks to the latter, we did not go hungry. Our attic was filled with runner beans, and potatoes were laid out all over the floorboards. We used to collect the wooden pallets that were used to transport Gloria milk cartons and placed them in the attic to spread out the potatoes, shallots and so on....we would sort through them and throw out anything that was rotten. We had rabbits, which had the advantage of reproducing quickly...those rabbits saved us. Meat ration tickets allowed my mother to make a hotpot on Sundays and the leftovers were used for Monday's hash.... after that, any other meat was rabbit.

We had friends who were farmers at Montmartin and they gave us butter. We were eight children, plus grandmother and the cousin. We managed to feed everyone without going too hungry, but it was a full-time occupation for my brother and my parents. The war was just about surviving and strafing. When the sirens sounded we dived under the tables. Several times a month we came under attack from British aircraft which attacked the railroads and stations. The British targeted the locomotives and strafed them. They would most often come in over the marches at tree-top level, attacking the locomotives. People were killed, including Madame Fortin. This family was really unlucky. Jean Fortin was killed in 1944 by a German shell when he was working for the STO obligatory labor service. Monsieur Fortin ran a café-bar in rue Torteron and his wife was kiled by a German shell in July 1944.

Carentan remained under German shell fire until 24 July 1944. The Germans fired on

These 501st Geronimos snatch some rest whilst they are photographed by the Signal Corps. (US Army)

Carentan everyday from Marigny. They were trying to stop US convoys from crossing the Saint-Hilaire bridge and a shell fell every three minutes. The Americans would wait for the three minutes to pass, then cross over. The list of civilian victims grew throughout July.

There were also resistance movements, ones which were essentially about collecting intelligence. There were not the right conditions to create a maquis. There was a fire at the Gloria factory in 1942. It supplied butter to the Germans and it was the butter section that burned down. We never knew whether it was due to an accident of resistance activity.

An increasingly severe occupation

The occupation along the coastal areas was particularly constraining and the men were often called up to work on the Atlantic Wall. The firefighters went to Sainte-Marie-du-Mont to help dig holes in the sand using the pressure of their pumps, in order to place obstacles. Every night, men patrolled along the roads to stop sabotage. We were very indifferent to the Germans. We felt humiliated, so we did not want to talk with them. My father would not have put up with it.

The Carentan area was very densely occupied. From the outset, the Germans expected an inva-

sion from England so they then concentrated on coastal defense. The Germans were respectful towards the population. They behaved well and, from 1942 onwards, even more so as they feared being sent to Russian and the Eastern Front in the event of any misdemeanor. They were, therefore, well-behaved.

Our only hope was for the British to come and we placed a lot of faith in Churchill. We expected a great deal from him, especially our liberation. It took us quite a while to understand that the Americans would be involved. We thought that the landings would take place in the north. On the Sunday before 6 June, we had taken our first communion and two of the girls who took it with us were killed as early as 10.00 on 6 June by a bomb. They were the Lamy family daughters and the entire family was killed. For me, 6 June is, therefore, a day of mourning.

These photos show 101st Airborne Division paratroopers using a tracked-motorbike (Kettenkrad) left behind by the Germans. The American paratroopers really liked this vehicle. (US Army)

Carentan at the heart of the fighting for liberation

From 6 in the morning onwards on 6 June 1944, Carentan was bombed by planes, notably around the station. A bomb fell on the Place de la République, hitting a wool shop and killing the owner. Then, at 13:30, a second air raid took place, targeting the Duval-Lemonnier fuel depot. Bombs fell on rue des Villas, where three families were hit, including the Lamy family. Two other families also lost members. This same raid killed the mayor of Carentan, Docteur Caillard. He was making his way along the road to Saint-Côme and was killed by a bomb blast from this raid.

Decorated with French and American colors, the Great War memorial in Place de la République, was the meeting point of the Division's 327th/401st Glidermen and paratroopers. (US Army)

At 7 in the morning we were told that landings were place. A lot of people wanted to leave. Our father said that there was no point in doing so as the battle would spread across the entire sector. He did not have a radio and it was not until Wednesday that the first news came in. Our neighbor had been to Saint-Hilaire and had seen American paratroopers at the wash house there! The presence of American paratroopers was quite a surprise to us! There was a lot of aerial activity. Docteur Simon worked with the nuns at the hospital where they took care of many wounded civilians. All the shopkeepers had left, apart from Binet, the baker at the corner of rue Torteron where, with his workers, he continued to make bread throughout the fighting. My father, who worked at the Gloria factory, had stolen some dried sausages that the Germans had stored there in the coolers. The Duval Lemonnier store had been bombed and there was quite a bit of foodstuff lying around there. Contrary to what has been said, the shops were not looted. People helped themselves, but they paid for it after the fighting. There we found a lot of soap, something that we had not been able to get during the entire war. My mother made her own soap using soot and soda! Whereas there had been soap at Duval Lemonnier.

We remained in the cellar of my grandmother's house that was set back a little from the road. On 11 June, the Germans pulled out of Carentan and started fires with phosphorous shells! The entire town could have burned down, but the firefighters fought the fires (see photos on page 102) by smothering them with sand. The Gloria factory burned a second time. We came under American artillery fire, particularly in rue Giesmard, notably on 12 June around 5 in the morning. Three shells hit the houses where we were. The entire gable of my grandmother's house was knocked down. My grandmother, who usually slept upstairs, had accepted to sleep in the cellar that night and it was this that saved her. My whole family survived without a scratch, whereas so many other families were totally wiped out, like the Lamy family. It was just a question of luck I suppose.

At around 7 am on 12 June, we saw Americans pass by, boys of the 327th GIR who entered the town via rue Giesmard. The joy we felt was unimaginable! I remember a huge American carrying a radio on his back. We had cartons of Gloria milk that were dented and unfit for sale, that my father bought at a knock-down price as a factory employee. The men fighting the fires passed by the house to drink this milk that helped them recover from the stench of the fires. We offered this milk to the Americans, who were very wary, but not of this Gloria milk, which had been bought by Americans, and the Gloria brand reassured them!

Free at last!

The first Americans did not have much to give us as they had nothing left themselves after a week of fighting. The next day, on 13 June, we were told to take down the flags as the Germans were back. It was at that point that my father decided to leave. We headed off towards Saint-Hilaire. We did not see any Americans as they were all fighting the SS on the outskirts of the town. There was a pontoon bridge between the Saint-Hilaire bridge and the railroad bridge. We came across the body of an American on the hill of Saint-Hilaire. We went to Monsieur Maillet at the Dumesnil farm near Saint-Pellerin. There was an American anti-tank unit positioned in front of the farm and we were scared that the Germans were coming back. At the end of the morning we heard tanks moving and the saw the arrival of the 2nd Armored. We were mad with joy. These tanks saved Carentan. We spent the night in the hay and an American artillery unit fired throughout the night in support of the defense of Carentan.

Carentan was of vital importance to the Germans who did all they could to take it back, shelling it right up to the end of July. The town paid a high price in destruction and civilian casualties. We returned there on 14 June and lived under the threat of German artillery, but life resumed its normal course. We watched convoys pass by and they would throw us chewing-gum, tins of food, chocolate and even oranges! This fruit was a rare thing until the liberation; it was something that we only got at Christmas, along with some barley sugar. It was the former Gloria boss, Madame Lécuyer, who gave them to my grandmother as she did her laundry. On 23 June, we went, along with my brother Louis, to the ceremony at the Place de la République [see following page]. We were late and we were running towards Place de la République when the first shells fell. We found shelter in Monsieur Chancet's shop, the butcher on rue Torteron. We hid in the corridor. Nineteen civilians were wounded and five of Carentan's inhabitants killed, including the toddler, Danièle Laisney, aged 4, who American medic, Bob Wright, could not revive.

Another vehicle taken by the Glidermen from German paratroopers, this time a *Kübelwagen*, close to the railroad crossing by the Holgate, on the highway to Saint Côme. (US Army

Danièle Laisney.

Three medal ceremonies were held in Place de la République on 15, 20 and 23 June 1944. That of 20 June was the most prestigious with the presence of Troy Middleton, when eleven 101st troopers received the Distinguished Service Cross for their actions in the liberation of Carentan. The young Danièle Laisney was present at the ceremony and she can be seen at the far left in the photo **above**.

Carentan became a logistical center for the Americans. In Place du Valnoble, there were huge depots of all sorts of things, notably oranges! There were American fire crews in rue Torteron, and African-American soldiers with whom we had snowball fights in the winter. Place du Valnoble was also an assembly point for American soldiers waiting for their units. We would go there on Sundays and chat with them. It was there that I met a young soldier from Boston, named Joseph Paradis, who spoke good French."

Opposite: Colonel Howard Johnson, CO of 501st PIR, receives a bouquet of flowers, in gratitude from the local population, from a young Carentan girl, watched by three other 101st regimental commanders, John Michaelis (502nd), Joseph Harper (327th) and Robert Sink (506th). This ceremony took place on Thursday 15 June and went down in history as the "4 Colonels Ceremony".

Above: Maxwell Taylor, CO of the 101st Airborne, awards the DSC to his four regimental commander, in the presence of the 327th GIR company.

THE KNIGHTS CROSSES OF THE "LIONS OF CARENTAN"

Facing the Screaming Eagles, von der Heydte's German parachutists fought valiantly and some were recipients of the prestigious Knight's Cross of the Iron Cross (*Ritterkreuz*), the foremost of these being its commander, *Major* and Baron, **Friedrich August von der Heydte**, who had seen action as a parachutist throughout all the campaigns (in the West, Crete and North Africa). He was awarded the *Ritterkreuz* on 9 July 1941. Captain **Horst Trebes** *(Kdr.* of *II battalion)* had also been in all the campaigns, including Crete, and he was awarded the *Ritterkreuz* on 9 July 1941; he was killed on 29 July 1944 at Saint-Denis-le-Gast. Lieutenant **Helmut Wagner**, fought in Holland and Crete, leading to the award of the *Ritterkreuz* on 24 January 1942 ; he was killed on 7 June 1944 at Saint-Côme-du-Mont by artillery fire. Captain **Rolf Mager** also fought in Crete and Italy, and went on to command *III./FJR 6*, he died of wounds on 1 January 1945. One NCO, *Oberfeldwebel* **Alexander Uhlig**, fought at Carentan and took over command of the 16th company when his commander was killed; he was awarded the *Ritterkreuz* on 29 October 1944 for having led a counter-attack at Carentan with 35 of his parachutists.

Georges Bernage

A view of the Place de la République during the 4 Colonels ceremony on 15 June.

Acknowledgments – Bibliography

This book sets out to be the synthesis of the best books written on the battle of Carentan.

I would like to give a big thank you to Mark Bando who, for nearly four decades, has recorded, conserved and shared the memories of the men who fought with the 101st Airborne Division. Today, the last men who took part in the battle of Carentan and in other 101st Airborne theaters of operations, are fading away. Mark Bando's attention to the smallest details is priceless. Ian Gardner has written no less than four books on the 3rd Battalion, 506th PIR. His knowledge is as great as his sunny disposition.
Thanks also to Michel Quilez for his precious help, Martin Long, Kate Jennings, Jeremy Payne and Lawrence Brown.

Ian Gardner - *Roger Day, Tonite we die as men*, Osprey, 2009.
Ian Gardner, *Airborne, the combat story of Ed Shames,* Osprey, 2015.
Kevin Brooks & Don Rich, *Glider Infantry man*, TAM, 2012.
Mark Bando, *The 101st Airborne at Normandy*, MBI, 1994.
Mark Bando, *101st Airborne, the Screaming Eagles at Normandy*, MBI, 2001.
Mark Bando, *Vanguard of the crusade*, The Aberjona Press, 2003.
Mark Bando, *Avenging Eagles*, Edwards Brothers Printing, 2006.
George Koskimaki, *D Day with the screaming Eagles*, Casemate, 1989.
Donald Burgett, *Currahee!*, Presidio, 1999.
Robert Bowen, *Fighting with the Screaming Eagles*, Greenhill Books, 2001.
Rapport&Northwood, *Rendez vous with Destiny*, The battery Press, 1948.
Clancy Lyall, *Siver Eagle*, Pneuma Springs Publishing, 2013.
Marshall SLA, *Night Drop*, Atlantic Monthly Press, 1962.
Robert J. Houston, *D Day to Bastogne*, Exposition Press, 1980.
Layton Black, *The last First Sergeant*, Griffith Publishing 1998.
Lawrence Critchell, *Four stars of Hell*, Ballantine Books, 1947.
James J. Sheeran, *No surrender*, Berkley Publishing, 2011.
Thomas M. Rice, *Trial by Combat*, Author House 2004.
Paul Woodadge, Angels of Mercy.
Charles H. Young, *Into the valley*, Printcom, 1995.
Gary N. Fox, *Graignes*, Gray Printing, 1990.
Tragedy at Graignes, Margaret & Dennis O'Leary, Universe books, 2011.
William True, *The cow spoke french*, Merriam Press, 2002.
G. William Sefton, *It was my war*, Sunflower University Press, 1994.
Francis Sampson, *Look out below, 101st Airborne Division Association*, 1958.
Thomas H. Taylor, *The simple sounds of Freedom*, Random House, 2002.
Gerald Devlin, *Paratroopper,* Robson Books, 1979.
Clay Blair, *Ridgway's paratrooper*, Naval Institute Press, 2002.
William B. Breuer, *Geronimo*, St Martin' Press, 1989.
Maxwell D. Taylor, *Swords and Plowshares*, Da Cap Press, 1972.
Matthew Pellett, *Last stop before Destiny*, 2014.
Matthew B. Ridgway, *Soldier*, Harper and Brothers, 1956.
Martin K A Morgan, *Down to earth,* Schiffer Military books, 2004.
Terry Poyser, *Fighting Fox Company*, Casemate, 2013.
John J. Maginnis, Military Government Journal, University of Massachusetts Press, 1971.
Robert K Wright Jr, John T. Greenwood, *Airborne forces at war*, Naval Institute Press, 2007.
Volker Griesser, *Les Lions de Carentan*, Heimdal, 2005.
Jerome Preisler, *Firts to Jump*, Berkley Publishing, 2014.
Michel De trez, *les casques parachutistes américains*, Histoire et Collections, 2014.

Photos: Rémi Martin

Printed in May 2019 by Drukarnia Skleniarz printers (Pologne),
for Editions Heimdal, Georges Bernage, publisher.